A188

A188

CLASSIC AIRCRAFT
in Aviation Art

STARTING UP
Vic McLindon

ROGER MARKMAN
CLASSIC AIRCRAFT
in Aviation Art

David & Charles

To Paul Berman

ACKNOWLEDGEMENTS

This book would not have been written but for my good friend Paul Berman, himself an established author and journalist, who encouraged me to pursue my 'good idea'. I am especially indebted to Geoffrey Lea to whom I owe much of my art education and who provided help with the introduction to this book. Thanks are also due to the British Guild of Aviation Artists, the American Society of Aviation Artists, and the Manchester Aviation Art Society for their help and co-operation. I would also like to thank Tri-Service Press for permission to quote from *The Narrow Margin*. Finally, thanks are due to Alison Elks of David & Charles. As I now know a book such as this is an amazingly complex product of the combined efforts of many specialists. Alison kept the whole show on the road, co-ordinating an array of inputs from many departments, including my own efforts.

The publishers would like to express their thanks to Commander Dennis White OBE, RN (ret) for his assistance during the production of this book.

A DAVID & CHARLES BOOK

Copyright © text Roger Markman 1993
Copyright © of all illustrations rests with the artist.
First published 1993

Roger Markman has asserted his right to be identified as author of this work in accordance with the Copyright, Designs and Patents Act 1988.

A catalogue record for this book is available from the British Library.

ISBN 0 7153 0046 6

Book designed by Michael Head

Typeset by Ace Filmsetting Ltd, Frome, Somerset
and printed in Singapore by C S Graphics Pte Ltd
for David & Charles
Brunel House Newton Abbot Devon

CONTENTS

Ivan Berryman
Born in Shoreham, Sussex in 1958 and now resident in the Isle of Wight, England, Ivan Berryman has been painting professionally since the late 1970s, quickly establishing an excellent reputation for his dramatic portrayals of aeronautical subjects of every kind.

Simon Bradshaw
Born in Manchester in 1956, Simon Bradshaw's interest in aviation began at an early age and has never wavered. He studied art at Rochdale College of Art in 1975, then photography at Manchester Polytechnic. Today he is a Senior Photographer with a leading advertising studio based in Manchester, England.

Gil Cohen
A member of the USAF Art Program, Vice-President and Artist Fellow of the American Society of Aviation Artists, Gil Cohen received the prestigious award 'Best of Show' in 1990 for his painting *Coming Home/England 1943*. His paintings reflect his interest in history and are sensitive portrayals of the human element set against the background of wartime airfield activity. Gil Cohen lives in Pennsylvania, USA.

Gerald Coulson
The work of Gerald Coulson is among some of the most familiar and best-loved in Britain today. His reputation in aviation art and landscape painting rests on his sensitivity and an ability to catch the realism of any scene. His first love was not art but aircraft, and his apprenticeship in the RAF has stood him in good stead, enabling him to paint from intimate knowledge. Gerald Coulson lives in Hertfordshire, England.

Richard Dann
Richard S. Dann grew up with a love of aviation. He earned his pilot's license whilst an aircraft engineer, and went on to join the US Navy, for whom he flew 50 combat missions during Operation Desert Storm. Richard has painted many aviation scenes for public and private commissions. He is a member of the American Society of Aviation Artists, and lives in Brookhaven, USA.

James Dietz
Following graduation from the Art Center College of Design in Los Angeles, Jim Dietz became a commercial illustrator, eventually settling in Seattle, USA, and specialising in aviation art. He not only portrays the hardware of flight, but also the human element, revealing the important interaction between man and machine.

Mark Franklin
Born in 1962, Mark Franklin attended Bournemouth & Poole College of Art & Design to study technical illustration. Since graduating in 1985 he has worked in London, England, as a freelance illustrator to a variety of advertising, design and publishing clients. The P-51 cutaway featured in this book reflects his personal interest in aviation.

David Hamm
Dave Hamm became a full-time artist after studying life painting for two years at Art College. He paints in both oils and watercolours. David Hamm lives in Hertfordshire, England.

Craig Kodera
Craig Kodera has always loved aviation. After graduation from UCLA he worked as a commercial artist, spending time at McDonnell Douglas Aircraft, where art and aviation merged. He spent many years in the Air Force Reserve, and while in the Air Rescue Service logged over 1,300 flying hours in the Lockheed HC-130H Hercules. Today he flies for American Airlines. He is Charter Vice-President of the American Society of Artists, his work hanging in several museums, and lives in California, USA.

Jim Laurier
Jim Laurier's interest in aviation began at a very early age. Later, he learnt to fly to broaden his understanding of aircraft and flight, piloting a P-51 Mustang to experience something of what World War II pilots went through. In his paintings he aims to convey the exhilaration of flight and reveal something of the 'soul' of the aircraft. Jim Laurier lives in New Hampshire, USA.

Geoffrey Lea
Geoff Lea took up oil painting whilst serving as a radio officer in the merchant navy, mostly landscapes and seascapes. He later extended his repertoire to include portrait work and military subjects, particularly aviation studies. He lives and works in Leeds, England.

Vic McLindon
Vic McLindon studied graphic design at Lancaster Polytechnic. He graduated in 1976 and entered a career in advertising. Today he combines a burgeoning illustration business with commissions for aircraft paintings, preferably American World War II types. He lives in Yorkshire, England.

Frank Munger
Leaving the RAF in 1945, Frank Munger joined the publishers of *Flight International* as editorial artist, retiring as chief illustrator in 1985. He started painting in the late 1940s with no formal art training. His subjects range is wide, but he specialises in early aviation and motoring, mostly painted in watercolour. Frank Munger is a member of the UK Guild of Aviation Artists and Associate Member of the Royal Aeronautical Society. He lives in Derbyshire, England.

Peter Newton
Peter Newton became a full-time aviation artist in 1975 and has been an Associate Member of the Guild of Aviation Artists since 1985, exhibiting and selling his work at the annual exhibition. In 1990 he won the British Aerospace Award for the best painting. Peter Newton lives in Sussex, England.

Peter Nield
Born in 1936 and educated at Oldham Hulme Grammar School, Peter Nield qualified as a Chartered Mechanical Engineer. A lifelong interest in aviation led naturally to involvement in aviation art. Peter is a founder member of the Manchester Aviation Art Society and prefers working in oils. He lives in Manchester, England.

Ernest Nisbet
A professional and graphic designer for the past twelve years following twenty years in banking, Ernest Nisbet's main activity is the design of postage stamps for the Crown Agents Stamp Bureau. He is also an Associate Member of the UK Guild of Aviation Artists and his work is exhibited regularly, selling on both sides of the Atlantic. He lives in Cheshire, England.

Mark Postlethwaite
Mark Postlethwaite is a professional artist painting exclusively aeronautical subjects. In 1987 he became the first artist in residence at the RAF Museum, Hendon and was elected to full membership of the UK Guild of Aviation Artists in 1991. He has paintings in private collections worldwide, in the RAF Museum collection, and on numerous RAF bases across the UK. He lives and works in Leicestershire, England.

Anthony Saunders
Born in Chelmsford in 1964, Anthony Saunders is a self-taught artist who has exhibited in many national exhibitions. He now runs his own publishing company based in Essex, England.

David Shepherd
Internationally celebrated as an artist and wildlife conservationist, David Shepherd is perhaps best known for his wildlife painting. He is, however, very popular as an aviation and locomotive painter, bringing a *joie de vivre* to all his work. His work has hung in the Royal Academy and is in keen demand in limited edition prints. David Shepherd lives in Surrey, England.

Robin Smith
Robin Smith took up painting in 1981 after a Fire Service accident forced early retirement. He learned to fly in 1968, but his painting soon took precedence. He is a member of the UK Guild of Aviation Artists, and lives in Lincolnshire, England.

Robert Taylor
Since becoming a professional painter in the mid 1970s, Robert has established himself as one of the world's most collected aviation artist. During the past five years his print editions have sold out on date of publication – a record achieved by few artists. Using a classic painterly style, Taylor achieves a rare combination of dramatic realism and aesthetic beauty that brings romance to a difficult, technical subject. Robert Taylor lives in Avon, England.

Charles J. Thompson
Born in India, the son of a British Army sergeant, Charles J. Thompson took early retirement eight years ago after thirty-seven years styling cars for Ford Motor Company. His painting now takes precedence. He is a full member of the UK Guild of Aviation Artists and an Artist Fellow of the American Society of Aviation Artists. He lives in Essex, England.

Michael Turner
Born in 1934, Michael Turner was fired with boyhood enthusiasm for aircraft and the exploits of the Royal Air Force. This continuing fascination with aviation found expression through painting. A founder member of the UK Guild of Aviation Artists, he has twice been Chairman and is currently President. He presently lives and works in Buckinghamshire, England.

Robert Watts
Robert Watts is an Artist Fellow of the American Society of Aviation Artists and ex-US Navy Combat Artist. He studied painting and design at New York's Pratt Institute and the Art Center School in Los Angeles. A professional illustrator for the past thirty years, he now devotes all his energies to the fine art of aviation from his home in California, USA. In 1992 he received the Best of Show award at the ASAA juried exhibition.

Ronald Wong
Ronald Wong is a self-taught painter who started out as a biochemist. He is a long-standing member of the UK Guild of Aviation Artists and has produced much work with the USAF in Britain as well as the RAF. He lives in Hertfordshire, England.

Frank Wootton
Frank Wootton studied at Eastbourne College of Art under Eric Ravilious. During World War II he worked as a war artist for the RAF, and his work hangs in museums and galleries throughout the world. He has held eight one-man exhibitions in Britain and America, and has received several awards for his contribution to aviation art. He lives in Sussex, England.

PREFACE

This is an unusual book, bringing together differing elements of art and analysis. Though there is much here to delight the art lover's eye, this is more than simply a collection of stunning paintings; the text aims to be informative in a way that will enhance the understanding of aviation art, and so increase the pleasure gained from it.

The introduction is intended to help you develop an 'eye' for art – to appreciate the subtleties of style and nuances of skill. As your 'eye' develops you will begin to notice all sorts of points, good and bad, in pictures both new and familiar. I do not claim any great expertise here; my comments are the result of viewing a great deal of aeronautical art, applying my mind to what I see in a constructively critical way, and talking to artists about their views on both their own work and that of others.

Many a child's first impression of classic aircraft was gained from a visit to the cinema, and a section of the introduction is devoted to this important aspect of aviation art. This takes the form of a general overview followed by a more detailed analysis of several influential films.

The rest of the book reviews six classic aircraft – Spitfire, Lancaster, B-17, Me109, P-51 Mustang and P-47 Thunderbolt. There are countless excellent books describing how these aircraft were powered and re-counting their wartime achievements, so I have tried to add something new, interesting and useful.

First, I consider the enduring popularity of these aircraft – what might be termed the 'sociology of aviation'. Some aircraft, especially perhaps the Spitfire and the Lancaster, have acquired an almost legendary status and this phenomenon is examined with the help of information drawn from the cinema, books, comics, model-making and many other areas of popular culture.

Second, I consider, in a very broad sense, the aesthetics of the aircraft. Some aircraft have a grace and line which is forever classic (the magnificent Spitfire with its thin elliptical wings for example), but many others are angular or just plain ugly. However, as with people, 'ugly' can equate with 'character' and 'interest'.

This quality of 'character' is also linked with nostalgia. These beautiful (or beautifully ugly) machines are masterpieces of design and craftsmanship evocative of a bygone, and some would say better, age. The sound of a piston aero engine has a soulful quality sadly lacking in this modern, high-tech era, comparable to that of a steam train, vintage car or grandfather clock. I doubt that today's products will ever evoke such fond memories! When viewing a really fine piece of aeronautical art you can almost hear the sound of the aero engines in the same way that a musician reading a score can 'hear' the music that is written down.

Third, I examine the history of the aircraft – and their aircrews – but not in the sense of a chronicle. Instead I attempt to analyse what historical aspects have caught the imagination of both artist and public alike: the fighter pilot as the knight of the air, the fighter plane his gallant steed; the B-17 waist-gunner as a metaphor for the gunner on a wooden battleship or the soldier at the battlement of a fort.

Nowadays, modern technology overshadows the human input. Computer-run wars may have their origins in World War II, but no guided missile will ever inspire in the same way as the Dam Busters.

Finally, a selection of paintings of each type of aircraft is discussed. I have tried to choose different interpretations of classic themes, such as speed, drama, excitement and beauty. Some of the artists themselves have some input to the text; they tell us what they were attempting and how successful they feel their interpretations have been.

In addition to the paintings, this book also contains a number of pencil sketches. The pencil sketch, sadly much ignored, is as valid and important a form of art as the oil painting. It exists alongside the black-and-white photograph as an art form which utilises tone rather than colour, conveying its message with equal, sometimes greater, effect.

Also included are three-view drawings and basic data on each aircraft, both for reference when viewing aeronautical art and to clarify scale effects when an aircraft is viewed against human figures. Of course one must make allowances for 'artistic licence'– the deliberate emphasising of such things as shape and size for effect – but note that artistic licence and error are *not* the same thing!

Also included is a cutaway illustration of the P-51 Mustang, to provide some 'anatomical' insight. Just as a good artist painting a nude needs to know some anatomy, so an aeronautical artist needs 'inside' knowledge of aircraft. This illustration will help you to appreciate the paintings and sketches as well as providing yet another example of the many forms aviation art can take.

I hope that you will enjoy owning this book as much as I enjoyed writing it, but, whatever your reactions, I will have achieved my aim if you are stimulated into thinking more critically when viewing an aeronautical, or indeed any artistic image.

MESSERSCHMITT Bf 109 G-14 *Simon Bradshaw*
11 × 16in (28 × 40.5cm), graphite pencil on paper.

Simon Bradshaw is an artist who specialises in pencil sketching. He has developed his technique to such a peak of perfection that his work must rate among the very best of its type. Needless to say, the production of a piece such as this takes the artist many hours of infinitely meticulous and painstaking work.

The immediate impression this picture creates is of an extremely solid nuts and bolts no-frills sort of warplane. In addition to the wealth of fine detail it is noteworthy how the artist has succeeded in reproducing the texture and effect of the different surfaces and materials. For instance, the rubber of the tyres looks quite different from the Perspex canopy or the metal propeller blades. It must always be remembered that in a picture such as this, the lightest light can only be the drawing paper itself. Given this fact, the glint of reflected light on the tailfin of the bomb is a quite remarkable touch.

The artist has posed the aircraft at an angle which serves to reinforce its rugged and purposeful shape. This is very much the mechanic's eye view, as he collects the tools or

equipment with which to start working on the aircraft. This is a picture in which one can lose oneself, allowing one's eye to wander all over the aircraft studying every fine detail of its construction, whilst also being able to draw back and admire the whole. The picture, depicting as it does the 109 flown by one of the outstanding fighter pilots of the war, Major Erich Hartmann, is a fitting tribute to a knight of the air as well as an historic fighter aircraft.

'Together with my fascination for aeroplanes, drawing them, it seems, has been a part of my life since childhood. The drawing itself is not a difficult task, as all the hard work has been done for me by the aircraft designers; my work serving merely as a testament to their abilities. Allied to this of course is the immense respect one builds up, not only for an individual aircraft, but also for the heroism of the pilots who flew them together with the countless numbers who maintain and cherish them.

I usually begin a drawing by researching as much detail as possible: each drawing may require at least twenty reference photographs, with information ranging from technical characteristics to historical information. A wide tonal range is essential if I am to reproduce faithfully the effects of light and shadow.

This will ultimately affect the dramatic aspect of the drawing.

Once the viewpoint has been decided, the drawing begins with rough outlines. Shading has then to be carefully pre-planned, working from light to dark, thus avoiding the chance of smudging. Pencils used range from 6H to 8B. As a pencil's characteristic changes when it becomes blunt, two pencils of the same lead-type are commonly used. A typical drawing may take in the region of 150 hours to complete, but is always a labour of love and never laborious.

The Messerschmitt Bf 109 is an impressive aeroplane. The one I have chosen to depict is that flown by Major Erich Hartmann of 11 Gruppe JG/52. With 352 confirmed victories to his credit, he is the world's highest-scoring fighter ace.'

SIMON BRADSHAW

WHAT IS AVIATION ART?

The purpose of this section is to pass on some useful hints and tips which will help you to develop a better 'eye' for aeronautical art. It is also hoped that it will help those who perhaps look *too* closely at the minutiae of technical/structural points to step back both mentally and physically to a position where they can appreciate the picture as an artistic composition.

ART AS STORY-TELLING

When viewing a painting, perhaps the first question to ask is 'What is the artist trying to say?' The answers to that simple question can be many and varied. The artist may be trying to say how incredibly fast the aircraft seems to be flying, how dramatic/exciting/horrific the air combat is, or how serene and beautiful is the scene portrayed. It is vital to ask this question and to glean some sort of answer. If a picture says nothing then it could be said that it is not a piece of art. It may be a wonderfully skilled illustration, and may be enjoyed as such, but it does not raise itself to the level of art.

Some would say that art falls short of its goal if it does not raise fundamental and vital questions about life, an argument which has been used to reduce representational art to the level of mere decorative home furnishings. This view has been dominant for much of the twentieth century, the rise of modern art leading to the almost total rejection of representational art by the major art institutions. This trend was encouraged by the mostly false assumption that Victorian representational art in particular was somehow smug, vulgar and shallow, and by the penchant for representational art of certain officials in both the Nazi and Stalinist regimes (under Stalin it was dubbed 'Socialist realism' in the USSR).

Now the trend is reversing and representational art, especially in fields such as aviation, is rising in popularity. This type of art has its origins in the highly moralistic Victorian world, and in particular in the military art of that time.

Many of the people who buy aviation art do so for its story-telling aspect. The types of story told are many and varied: some pictures depict the excitement, drama and horror of air combat while others evoke the fun and nostalgia of flying – the brightly coloured pre-war biplane looping the loop, for instance. Art need not be all anguished self-examination. It can be, and often is, pure entertainment – the equivalent of a good novel or film. Lovers of the story-telling aspect of aviation art will always be keen to know the 'what', 'where', 'when' and 'who' of the picture.

Having decided *what* the artist is trying to say, we can now go on to examine *how* the message is conveyed.

COMPOSITION

Composition refers to how the artist has put together the different elements in the picture. Composition can enhance perspective – the illusion of depth is produced partly by the converging of lines to a vanishing point and partly by good composition. For example, a carefully spaced formation of aircraft behind the main subject will create a much greater sense of reality than a closely bunched group. Similarly, on-the-ground scenes are enhanced if figures are placed behind and in front of aircraft.

Composition also refers to the overall geometric shape produced by the elements in a picture. One classic composition is a triangle. This was much loved by the old masters and is very much more pleasing to the eye than many other arrangements.

A good artist uses composition and a degree of artistic licence to enhance perspective, realism and general interest. Trees and clouds should harmonise with and enhance the overall composition; indeed all minor subjects, such as other aircraft, people, equipment, buildings, vehicles, etc, should never be randomly scattered. Artists take great care when using photographs as reference material. Exact copying of photographs is unwise as they are rarely well composed.

DISTANCE

Another fundamental rule of representational art is that a painting should appear to have depth of field; thus objects further away should appear so, with a distinct difference between foreground, middle distance, and background.

Distance does not only mean objects should appear smaller – colours become softer and more subdued, some dark tones become lighter and light tones become darker, reducing the overall contrast. It is not necessary to look at pictures to appreciate this – next time you are in the countryside, notice how the colour and sharpness of the landscape varies with distance. Dust in the air and other atmospheric effects such as high moisture content can refract (bend) light, filter certain colours and generally interfere with what we see to produce often very dramatic effects. This is familiar to those who live in sight of hills or mountains. On a clear, windy day these will be seen with pin-sharp clarity compared to days when the air is laden with dust or pollutants.

Some poorly constructed pictures exhibit 'cylindrical' land, in which the land appears to curve dramatically away from you. Another problem is that of 'wallpaper' land, in which lack of adequate perspective means that the land appears to be flat and one-dimensional. Whether the horizon is painted on a slant, high in the picture, or low down the painting, the artist needs to use a combination of perspective and colour to ensure a realistic representation of landscape stretching into the distance.

SPEED AND ACTION

Flying is at its most dramatic when there is some feeling of speed, and so also is aviation art. Aeronautical artists employ a variety of techniques in order to bring a sense of speed to their work. One method, which can be very effective, is to construct perspective both in the land below and in the sky. Perspective helps to convey speed by creating the illusion that the subject is almost explod-

'Stromberg Carburettors' advert. Engine component manufacturers used images suggesting air power very effectively.

ing out of the picture from the vanishing point. It is often used in aviation art to great effect. In the case of aircraft shown above cloud, the perspective is in the cloud below the aircraft. This can be further emphasised by slightly blurring the cloud and/or land. Another method is to blur part or all of the aircraft. This is rarely as successful as blurring the background.

Speed lines coming off rudders and wing-tips are also used by some. These streaks were much loved by commercial artists portraying trains and aircraft in the early part of the twentieth century, and were often incorporated into the airline liveries which appeared on the actual aircraft. They can, unfortunately, look artificial if not used with great skill.

Exhaust gases, smoke and/or condensation trails help to suggest speed if used in moderation. Condensation trails are produced by the freezing of water vapour in the exhaust of both piston and jet-engined aircraft.

This phenomenon only occurs at altitudes of about 20,000ft and higher.

Wing-tip vortices are clearly distinguishable from speed lines. Vortices are essentially miniature clouds, streams of condensed water vapour, and as such are much the same colour as clouds. At the wing-tips where they appear there is usually a kink or wave as they form before they trail off behind. They are produced by high speed and 'G' loading. Speed lines are most often shown as being the same colour as the aircraft and are numerous and short (shorter than the length of the fuselage), looking quite unlike wing-tip vortices.

Ironically, aircraft are often portrayed 'at speed' when flying at their slowest; that is, on take-off (a fighter scramble, for instance, is a much-loved subject for aeronautical artists). It is interesting to note that a Spitfire could take off at about the same speed as a modern family car can cruise down a motorway!

THE PROPELLER

The depiction of the propeller is a much-discussed topic in aeronautical art circles. Spinning propellers tend to be invisible, so to improve safety on the ground most air forces introduced coloured propeller tips – yellow was used in the Royal Air Force and the Royal Navy. Light is reflected by the painted tips and produces a faint circle. Propeller blades were often painted matt black to prevent glare distracting the pilot, leaving only the coloured tips of the rotating propeller visible. When viewed at a slight angle the propeller disc (which becomes an ellipse in half-profile) should cast partial shadows from the blades.

Insofar as there are rules for the depiction of a spinning propeller, a good artist should follow them. First, there is the geometry of the ellipse. The propeller disc of an aircraft seen other than head-on should be elliptical. The centre line of the propeller forms the axis about which the major and minor chords are constructed. Second, there is the depiction of the disc itself. Stroboscopic effects produced by photography and video can 'freeze' propeller blades or produce shadows which would not normally be seen. A skilfully painted propeller disc is a subtle and beautiful piece of art in its own right which avoids the pitfalls of photographic reproduction. Even painted propellers will often catch and reflect light, and where this does not occur then blurring of the aircraft structure seen through the disc will. Finally, the blade tips will often be seen as part streaks of colour which add to the feeling of speed and power.

THE LENS EFFECT

People have a tendency to regard photographs and paintings quite differently. A photograph taken with a wide-angle lens will produce an image very different from the same scene viewed with the naked eye – a phenomenon known as the lens effect. Simply because it is a photograph, however, it will tend to be seen as an accurate depiction. A painting or drawing, on the other hand, is often viewed much more critically. A photograph exhibiting the lens effect would look quite wrong if copied on to canvas, and such slavish copies of camera images are usually easy to spot as a result.

The distortions of what seems like a representational photograph can be easily demonstrated by tracing a 'good' photograph on to paper. It will often look quite unnatural when transferred in this way. Artists need to exercise careful judgement when working from photographs in order to make their work appear accurate to the observer. Common results of failure to do so are that the wing nearest the viewer seems too long, or the wings and tailplane seem to taper too sharply to the vanishing point. Often these two surfaces are better adjusted to near-parallel. Once possessed of this insight, paintings copied directly from photographs will become increasingly obvious.

COLOUR

Colour is, to a large extent, a matter of personal taste. American aeronautical art is characterised by very bright, strongly contrasted, sharply lit images. This may be connected with the American climate, especially in the west where strong sunlight and blue skies abound. British artists often favour soft autumnal tones and weaker diffuse sunlight, which reflect Britain's climate.

As an artistic principle warm colours, for example red and orange, tend to stand out in a painting while blues and greens, which are cooler, recede into the painting. Colour is used by artists to enhance both depth and perspective.

Clouds are a major feature of many aviation paintings, and their skilful depiction lies to a large extent in a subtle use of colour. No cloud is pure white – they possess a multitude of colour, which can be adapted to create a specific mood or dramatic effect. Pure white is a colour which is used sparingly by most artists; they use it only for the strongest highlights, often in very small measure. Black is also used with care. A solid black runway, for instance, will divert the viewer's attention away from the aeroplane. Again, used sparingly it can greatly improve a picture by adding depth and enhancing any darker blues and greens.

Colours interact in subtle ways partly because of the effects of light and partly because of the way in which our brains interpret them. A skilled artist uses these effects to create 'mood' – a major element in style; for example, certain lighter or darker tones, when placed next to a given area of colour, affect our perception of that area – perhaps making it seem lighter or darker, nearer or farther away. This effect is partly optical (the interference of the light rays), and partly psychological.

LIGHT

All natural light comes from the sun – even moonlight is reflected sunlight. Consequently, in a painting, the *principal* source of light should usually come from one direction.

It is easy to test for this consistency. Look for a patch of reflected light on, for example, a cockpit canopy. This represents light from the principal source reflecting out of the picture at right angles to the canvas. The angle of the reflecting surface will tell you where the artist has placed the principal source of light. All other reflecting surfaces should indicate light from the same source; if not the picture will seem odd. This is one point where photography (in natural light) and art match up perfectly. A good artist *must* get the lighting correct.

Secondary sources of light, mostly reflections of the primary source, can complicate matters slightly; however, the same basic principles apply.

A technique which can backfire if the artist is not exceptionally skilled is the use of pre-painted skyscapes as backdrops on to which aircraft are painted. This technique often gives itself away because the painting's lighting is unbalanced. A painting should generally be built up as a whole to ensure that the entire composition is correctly lit. It is interesting to note how many pictures which somehow seem just that little bit unsatisfactory often slot into this category.

MEDIA

Despite the wonders of modern material technology, 'oil on canvas' is still as popular as it was four hundred years ago. An oil painting on canvas will probably still command the highest price, all other things being equal.

An oil painting has great texture, as a result of the grain of the canvas and the technique of applying the paint; this produces wonderful, glowing, three-dimensional effects. A print of an oil painting – ultimately ink on paper – can never reproduce the effects of the original.

Acrylic paint, essentially a plastic, can be used much as oils, but being very fast-drying cannot be reworked as oils can. Some artists prefer acrylics to oils, but the majority consider that oils can produce more subtle and soft tones and textures.

To complicate matters there is also alkyd, which is a hybrid acrylic/oil paint. Like acrylic paint, it uses resin as a base, but the pigment used is the same as in oil paint. Alkyd works as a very fast-drying oil paint, which combines the properties of both media.

Oil paints have remained virtually unchanged for centuries and have been used by the finest painters. However, modern technology is constantly developing and improving the colour and feel of acrylics, and many contemporary artists are finding their properties very suited to their style and approach.

Aeronautical artists work in many and varied media. Which one is preferable is largely a matter of taste, although oils can probably produce the widest range of effects.

STYLE

Style can express itself in a variety of ways. Some artists' style is most evident in their composition. Dramatic battle and action scenes full of movement and excitement can be an instantly recognisable 'signature'. Other artists, often British, may be recognised by their mellow, soft, subtle use of colour, often coupled with a love of landscape. Many American artists favour vivid, sharp, contrasting colours and the intense, cloudless skies commonly found in many parts of the USA. There are artists who love to show the aircraft in finely detailed close-up, and yet others who prefer to paint the aircraft almost into the background.

Style is as much a feeling for the subject as anything else, and how a subject is portrayed often reflects the artist's inner feelings. Within a short while it will become quite easy to recognise different artists' work. The pictures reproduced in this book provide a chance to compare styles for yourself.

CONCLUSION

The purpose of this chapter has been to help you to develop an 'eye' for art by outlining some of the basics. With a little knowledge and a genuine love of the subject, your appreciation of art will develop through

This Boeing advertisement captures the feeling of the time – victory through air power.

time. You will quite possibly see as much 'bad' art as good, but remember that experts are people who know how to break rules which they are masters of. They must not be confused with those who break the rules simply because they are unskilled. It is well worth learning how to tell the difference between them.

AVIATION ART AND THE CINEMA

In this chapter we shall consider those factors which make aviation films such a powerful medium for the stimulation of artist and enthusiast alike, and then look at specific films which relate to those classic aircraft featured later in the book.

Aviation films have always fired the imagination of enthusiasts. They are a major source of inspiration for aviation artists, providing the imaginative stimulation necessary for the creative process to come to fruition. Many artists can trace their lifelong fascination with aircraft back to the time when, as a child, they saw a particular film.

Manned flight and commercial moving pictures are of approximately equal age. The Wright brothers were filmed by the first generation of movie cameras for the early newsreels. Greater numbers of people saw an aeroplane on the screen in those pioneering days than ever saw one flying overhead. It was not until the 1960s that air travel became affordable to the masses. Before then, for the vast majority, the only experience of flying and aeroplanes was to be had in the cinema.

Over the years there have been cinematic milestones that stand out as classics of their genre. Undoubtedly one of the most outstanding films in terms of the authenticity of the aerial sequences, explosions etc (there were few special effects) was Howard Hughes' *Hells Angels*, made in 1931. Doubtless it inspired many impressionable young lads to join the fledgling Army Air Corps or Royal Air Force.

In the pre-TV era, the cinema was an immensely powerful medium. Uninterrupted by advertisements, the large screen in a darkened theatre held sway over the minds and imagination of millions. This power was used to great and terrible effect by the Soviet and Nazi German film industries who both produced aviation-oriented propaganda films. In the Allied democracies the term 'morale boosting' was used, and many such aviation films were made during World War II.

The aircraft featured in this book were all film stars in their own right during and after World War II. These films have nearly all survived, and those made by Hollywood and the British film industry are regularly televised. Wartime 'morale boosting' documentaries and training films are now to be found on video. The German newsreels, documentaries and feature films are much less readily available. Some have 'surfaced', but many German aviation films are still in archival limbo.

Seeing *The Dam Busters* as a nine-year-old is one of my most vivid memories of childhood and one I undoubtedly share with many others. The artist Gil Cohen, at a similar age but some years earlier, was equally enthralled by *Air Force* and today, over fifty years on, is still inspired to paint B-17s, the 'star' of that film.

Whether or not you are an aviation film buff, this book will help you to view your next aviation film with an educated naïvety. By this apparent contradiction in terms I mean educated in the sense of having a deeper knowledge of the aircraft concerned, but naïve in that you will more easily be able to identify with the lives and times of the characters portrayed. Perhaps then you might taste the stuff of inspiration that motivates the aviation artist.

The Spitfire on film

The First of the Few
MELBOURNE/BRITISH AVIATION, 1942
DIRECTOR: LESLIE HOWARD

The Spitfire legend had been established during the Battle of Britain in 1940. Being such a beautiful little aeroplane, and such a delight to see in flight, it immediately caught the public's imagination. By the time *The First of the Few* came to be made the legend was already established; in a way, this film set the seal on it for ever.

As with *The Dam Busters*, *The First of the Few* also revolves around the boffin and the airman. In this case, the boffin was R. J. Mitchell, the young gifted designer doomed to a premature death, and the airman a fictional RAF fighter-type. The former was played brilliantly by Leslie Howard, himself destined to fall to the guns of a Luftwaffe fighter, and the latter by David Niven.

The film opens with genuine RAF fighter pilots discussing the Spitfire in now wonderfully dated British public-school accents. The story of the transition from Schneider Trophy racing seaplane to Spitfire is illustrated with fascinating sequences re-enacting the building and flying of the Spitfire prototypes.*

The film is pure fantasy from beginning to end, but is based on fact and combines actual film footage shot in battle and test flying with staged and recreated incidents to create a kind of meta-reality, the one being virtually indistinguishable from the other. Now sufficiently aged to be enjoyed with a warm glow of nostalgia, this film is a celebration of all things 'decent' and 'British', in particular the quintessentially British Spitfire.

Reach for the Sky
RANK, 1956
DIRECTOR: LEWIS GILBERT

This film, essentially a 'biopic', tells the story of Douglas Bader. As a legless Battle of Britain fighter pilot, he became a legend in his own lifetime and an inspiration to millions everywhere. Just as Richard Todd 'became' Gibson so too did Kenneth More virtually become Douglas Bader. Both actors apparently made a major study of the men they were to play.

Only a relatively small part of this film deals specifically with the Battle of Britain (shortly following which Bader became a prisoner-of-war). It is nevertheless a film centred very much around the Spitfire. There is

---

* The Schneider Trophy was donated by Frenchman Jacques Schneider in 1913 to be presented annually to the fastest seaplane over a 350km course. Any country winning the trophy three times in five years would retain it – a feat that Great Britain achieved on 13 September 1931, so ending the series. The trophy is on display at the Royal Aero Club, London

some good footage of aerial combat and an assortment of veteran 'Spits' fly again.

The film successfully established Kenneth More as a top British actor. Appearing as it did in the mid-1950s it also helped to establish the post-war fascination with the Battle of Britain and the Spitfire.

The Battle of Britain
UNITED ARTISTS, 1969
DIRECTOR: GUY HAMILTON

By the time this film was made the modern nostalgia industry was firmly established. Plenty of lovingly re-stored aircraft were brought together for the filming, which at its height rivalled *Hells Angels* for sheer num-bers in the air. The Me109s in the film were flown by the Confederate Air Force – an American club formed by veteran pilots and other enthusiasts to collect and maintain World War II aircraft. Theirs is the largest flying collection of such aircraft in the world and numbers some eighty machines, including Spitfires, Me109s, B-17s, Mustangs and many others.

This highly spectacular aviation film is historically very accurate, its length enabling the portrayal of real-istic chronological sequences and detail from the fall of France in the early summer of 1940 through to the end of the battle late in the year.

William Walton was commissioned to write a piece of music, 'Battle in the Air', and even the souvenir bro-chure had a foreword by Lord Dowding himself (Com-mander of Fighter Command in the Battle of Britain) and a letter from Prince Philip. The cast included many top names from the ranks of the British acting establish-ment: Dowding was played by Laurence Olivier; Kenneth More a 'flier' again.

Often televised, the film remains the definitive British statement on the Battle. This epic, big-budget, star-studded production is certainly worth seeing and is a source of continuing inspiration for artists.

The Lancaster on film

The Dam Busters
ASSOCIATED BRITISH PICTURE CORPORATION, 1954
DIRECTOR: MICHAEL ANDERSON

This was an enormous hit when it went on general release in 1955 and its theme tune, 'The Dam Busters

The poster of the 1954 film *The Dam Busters*.

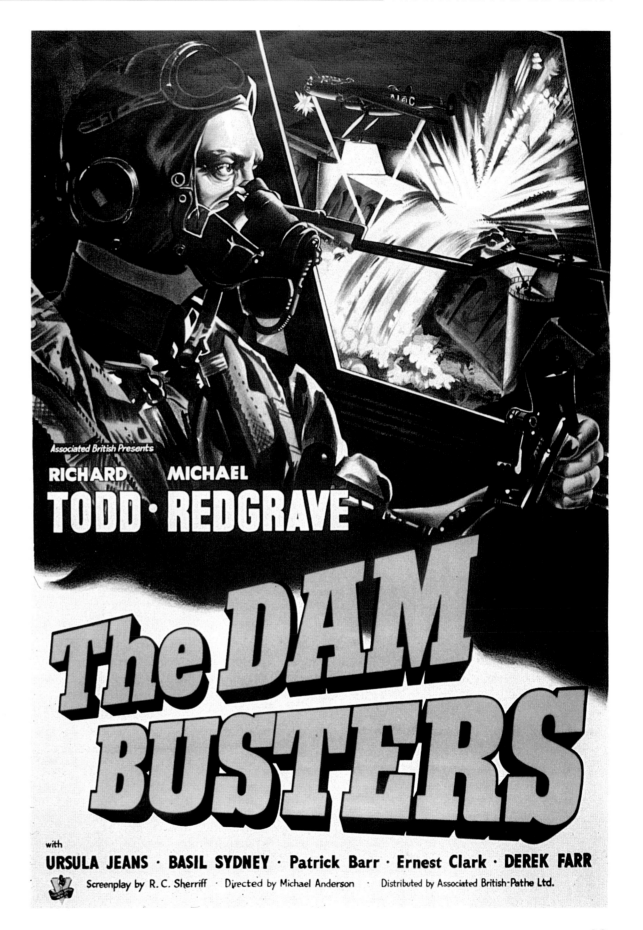

March' by Eric Coates, remains a standard, played frequently by RAF and other bands at air shows. Dominating the film is Richard Todd's portrayal of Guy Gibson, leader of 617 Squadron, known thereafter as 'The Dam Busters'. A brilliant foil to Todd's Gibson is Michael Redgrave as Barnes Wallis; portrayed as the archetypal British boffin battling interminably with officialdom for acceptance of his ideas.

The impact of this film in Britain was so powerful that the theme tune became, unofficially, the RAF march and the entire Dam Busters story entered into the realms of British folklore along with Trafalgar and Waterloo. Paul Brickhill's book of the same name on which the film was largely based, and Guy Gibson's own account, *Enemy Coast Ahead*, have never been out of print. Undoubtedly this film will continue to cast its spell on future generations.

The film portrays the Lancaster very well. For the actual shooting three were used (and later scrapped!). The aircraft's wonderful shape is set off well with fine camera angles, and the imaginative use of both engine noise and music produce a feeling of tension and drama.

In contrast to the relatively spacious interior of the B-17, the Lancaster was a cramped aircraft, and this feeling of almost fighter-like compactness inside the fuselage comes across well in the film.

As a military and engineering achievement, the Dam Busters' raid ranks among the greatest of all time. Perhaps this is why postcards of the breached dam are still on sale to tourists who come to see the site of this staggering feat. The massive repair work to the dams, carried out in a different-coloured concrete, stands as a silent witness to the extent of the devastation wrought.

Along with the Spitfire, the Lancaster has become a part of the British heritage and this film contributed greatly to that process. As a consequence, the Lancaster has inspired innumerable paintings and is second only to the Spitfire as the most popular subject for British aviation artists.

The B-17 Flying Fortress on film

Air Force
WARNER BROTHERS, 1943
DIRECTOR: HOWARD HAWKS

The dust had scarcely settled at Pearl Harbor when Warner Brothers decided to make *Air Force*, an all-action 'gung ho' drama which tells the story of a B-17C and its crew caught up in the opening stages of the Pacific war. Island-hopping across the Pacific they suffer numerous forced landings, fight countless battles with swarms of enemy fighters and finally sink half a Japanese task force, thus thwarting an invasion!

The story is pure comic-book stuff but the movie is redeemed by several other factors. The acting is very good, especially that of the great John Garfield. The aerial photography – in contrast with the not very special effects – is excellent, due in no small measure to the flying of veteran Hollywood movie pilot Paul Mantz. The interior flight sequences are very good and established, perhaps slightly before the historical reality, the B-17's legendary status as a flying gunship. Thus before the *Memphis Belle* had crossed the Atlantic audiences were treated to the delights of B-17 firepower downing Zeros, cascading brass shellcases and the trauma of combat. Never before or since has Hollywood so accurately portrayed an aerial battle before it actually happened. The heroism, battle-damage and forced landings are here, just as in the actual battles that were about to occur in the skies over Europe.

At the time of its release the film had a tremendous impact on at least one budding aviation artist: ten-year-old Gil Cohen was spellbound and his love affair with the B-17 continues undimmed by time. *Air Force* lives on through video and TV and may well inspire others to paint B-17s in the next century.

Memphis Belle
WAR ACTIVITIES COMMISSION, 1943
DIRECTOR: WILLIAM WYLER

This film, shot entirely on location at a B-17 base in England, is an early example of war documentary film-making. Like *Air Force* it is the story of one particular B-17, the *Memphis Belle*, and its crew. The similarity is so striking that William Wyler may well have been inspired by the earlier film. *Memphis Belle* was shot on 16mm film as the cameras were much less bulky than the usual 35mm format and permitted shooting in otherwise inaccessible situations. The film was made in colour, a new technology at the time.

The film lays great stress on the technological aspects of this type of warfare. The peace of the timeless, idealised English countryside with its thatched cottages and tranquil landscape is contrasted with the hive of industry that is the bomber base. Central is the aircraft with its then ultra-modern engines, equipment – maintained and crewed by highly trained specialists. To audiences still mindful of the trenches, this type of warfare must have seemed almost like science-fiction.

The raid was, as normal for B-17s, a daylight one and as such was hazardous. The anti-aircraft guns could see their targets and so could the deadly single-engined day fighters of the Luftwaffe. Protective fighter escort for the entire raid was not possible and over the target, the most vulnerable stage of all, no escort would be available. (Later in the war fighter escort could be provided throughout.)

The bombing run over the target was the most nerve-wracking stage of the raid as the aircraft would have to fly straight and level for several minutes, making themselves virtual sitting targets. After all the bombs were released the formation could turn for home and collectively take evasive action. The USAAF policy of daylight bombing, much riskier than the RAF night offensive, had the benefit of great accuracy. The American airmen were very proud of the Norden bombsight fitted to the B-17s, which enabled extremely precise bombing.

The raid featured in this film was against industrial and military targets: factories and U-boat pens. Each stage is recorded from planning and briefing to touchdown. All the aerial sequences are real; when we see gunners firing, fighters attacking, bombs falling, we are watching history in the making.

Great personal courage was involved in the making of this film. Apart from the obvious dangers involved in flying on a raid, the film crew, had they been captured, risked being shot as spies. This was especially true of William Wyler who was also Jewish.

The film is a marvellous resource for all aviation enthusiasts and artists. Anyone attempting to paint B-17s in battle would do well to refer to it at some point, and even ground details are shown in sufficient detail to provide key reference data. It is, of course, also a source of inspiration and a unique record of the time.

The *Belle* survived the war and is now a major tourist attraction in Memphis, Tennessee. It is one of the most painted, and probably the most famous, B-17 of all time.

Catherine Wyler, William Wyler's daughter, made the following points to me about *Memphis Belle*:

As far as I know, my father made the documentary *Memphis Belle* to show people at home what young American flyers were doing in the Army Air Corps in England. He joined the Air Force to help the war effort by making movies. Sent to make a documentary about B-17s, he realised during the shooting that the *Memphis Belle* would probably be the first plane to complete twenty-five missions (although we now know that is in question), so he focused on the *Belle* and her crew.

Memphis Belle is to my mind a near-perfect documentary, because it tells the story in a very cinematic fashion, and uses music and a beautiful narration to give added drama to the whole. Its universality and its ability to move audiences fifty years after it was produced show what an extraordinary achievement it is.

Memphis Belle
WARNER BROTHERS, 1990
DIRECTOR: MICHAEL CATON-JONES

The idea to produce a remake of *Memphis Belle* was that of Catherine Wyler – the late William Wyler's daughter – who saw it as a great opportunity to tell the amazing story of that aircraft and its crew. The film is both an historical record and a monument to the crew and her father. Although fictionalised, all the major incidents in the film actually happened, though not all on the one raid as shown.

The making of the film was itself an aviation event. Catherine Wyler, who co-produced the film with David Putman, said of the filming:

The structure of the film seemed to lend itself to a fictionalised treatment of the story. It was very self-contained, but also very dramatic, a wonderful starting point for a feature film.

Perhaps the most dramatic moment for me during the re-making of *Memphis Belle* came before the actual shooting even began. It was the day that the *Sally B* went to escort the two B-17s arriving from France back to Duxford. I was waiting on the tarmac when suddenly loudspeakers announced that three B-17s – the largest contingent to fly over England since World War II – were about to appear on the horizon. It was a Saturday, and since Duxford is the home of the Royal Air Force Museum, the usual weekend crowd was viewing the exhibits. Moments later, flying in perfect formation, the planes appeared and we all went crazy. It was enormously exciting to think that I had caused this memorable event, and I was only sorry that my father wasn't there to see it. The next three weeks were spent on the aerial photography for the movie. We often had seventeen planes in the air: B-17s, Mustangs, Messerschmitts and the camera plane. The planes had come from all over Europe and their multilingual pilots and engineers were a rakish bunch. They performed admirably, but we were thankful when the complicated manoeuvres finally ended without a hitch.

In the summer of 1943, a fierce battle raged across the skies of Europe. Ten brave young men flew on the wings of victory.

Memphis Belle

An extraordinary adventure.

WARNER BROS. Presents
an ENIGMA PRODUCTION "MEMPHIS BELLE" Starring MATTHEW MODINE
ERIC STOLTZ and JOHN LITHGOW Music by GEORGE FENTON Written by MONTE MERRICK
Produced by DAVID PUTTNAM and CATHERINE WYLER Directed by MICHAEL CATON-JONES
Association with BRITISH SATELLITE BROADCASTING and COUNTY NATWEST VENTURES

We worked very hard to make the movie as realistic and technically perfect as possible. We especially wanted the men who flew in those planes to appreciate the film and to feel that it demonstrated their part in the war to their children and grandchildren.

Once again the aircraft is the real star with its sleek, timeless beauty, its superb engines and its spartan 1930s art deco-like interior. The cast recreate the tone of the 1940s exactly. This is perhaps not surprising as they all attended a week's 'Bootcamp' to produce just this effect.

Although *Air Force* and this film are separated by nearly fifty years, it is interesting to note that they both have the same basic structure with similar character types, situations and actions. The World War II aviation movie is in many ways a sort of aerial western; as a genre it will probably last just as long.

The 1990 poster from the remake of *Memphis Belle*, originally filmed in 1943.

Twelve o'clock High
20TH CENTURY-FOX, 1949
DIRECTOR: HENRY KING

Made shortly after the war this film was destined for a role unimagined by its creators. So well did Gregory Peck portray the new base commander determined to improve morale and efficiency that the movie became a training aid both for officer cadets in the British Army and in industry as well! This speaks volumes for the film's authenticity and quality, at least from the military organisational point of view.

Much original footage is interspersed with sequences shot using B-17s, again (as in *Air Force*) flown by Paul Mantz. Drawing inspiration from William Wyler's

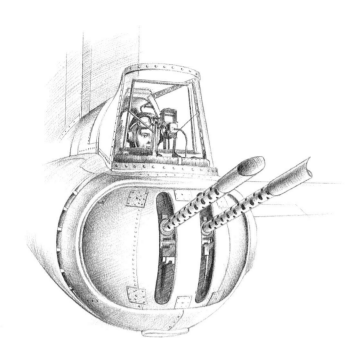

B-17 gunner
Vic McLindon

authentic footage, the film stresses the leadership aspect of aerial war and the interpersonal relationships that develop – a far cry from the comic-book plot of *Air Force*. As well as being an outstanding film of the genre it is also excellent artistically.

The P-51 Mustang on film

Empire of the Sun
ROBERT SHAPIRO, 1987
DIRECTOR: STEVEN SPIELBERG

Steven Spielberg, the now legendary Hollywood film-maker, clearly has a great feeling for aircraft and they feature in many of his films.

In the superb *Empire of the Sun*, based on the autobiographical novel by J. G. Ballard, aircraft figure prominently. The young hero of the film is obsessed with flying and, although a prisoner of the Japanese, admires their air force. As an air base with Zero fighters adjoins

his prison camp, he has ample opportunity to indulge his plane-spotting hobby. This being World War II he is treated to some spectacular air shows courtesy of the US and Japanese air forces.

In one memorable scene a P-51 Mustang on a strafing mission flies over our hero. The shot is in slow motion, the cockpit hood is slid back, and as our hero is on the flat roof the plane is almost at eye level. At that moment the pilot waves!

Several aviation enthusiasts I have spoken to found this moment overwhelming. So did I! In that instant the film captures the essence of the pilot as a knight. The concept of chivalry and the fighter pilot may have begun with the Red Baron but it did not end there. Ally that to the P-51 Mustang and you have one of the most powerful images of aviation ever screened – all within a matter of seconds.

The film is heavy on chivalrous imagery and much is made of saluting – the boy and Japanese fighter pilots; American servicemen, etc. Moreover, these 'saluting scenes' place strong emphasis on the deeply felt emotional/belief system implicit in that action. It is not mere form.

Like many of Spielberg's outstanding films, *Empire of the Sun* strikes a very deep chord indeed. It has certainly fired the imagination of many aviation enthusiasts and artists and will no doubt continue to do so.

The P-47 Thunderbolt on film

Thunderbolt
MONOGRAM PICTURE CORPORATION, 1947
DIRECTOR: WILLIAM WYLER

Following his success with *Memphis Belle*, William Wyler went on to make an equally impressive film about Thunderbolts and their pilots. Shot in Italy, this film too was in colour and on 16mm stock.

As the P-47 was a single-seat aircraft, a way had to be devised to shoot the film without a cameraman aboard. Cameras were rigged up in the cockpit, undercarriage, wheel-wells, and virtually anywhere else they would fit, to be set in motion either automatically or by the pilot. Some truly amazing footage resulted. Catherine Wyler said of this film:

Thunderbolt was a documentary which had a huge impact on my father and his family, because it was during the shooting of that film that he was deafened in one ear. It happened after he spent some hours next to the pounding engines of a plane on a mission. He was completely deaf for a couple of weeks, after which the hearing came back partially in one ear, so that, thankfully, he was able to continue his career as a director. My father was forty when he joined the Air Force, and he always believed that his going deaf was partially due to the fact that he was so much older than everyone else.

Like *Memphis Belle*, *Thunderbolt* was not a cinema feature as such but was widely shown to service and civilian audiences. It has more recently been born anew on video. This is a superb example of film-making and was an outstanding innovation in its day. It is a truly fabulous store of action sequences, and as such is of tremendous interest. ·

The Me109 on film

Whenever German aircraft were required in war films made after World War II there were two often-used solutions to the problem of obtaining flying 109s. One was to use the Me108, a similar-looking aircraft built after the war in Switzerland. The wings and tail very closely resembled the 109 but the fuselage was rather fatter to accommodate two side-by-side seats. Nevertheless, suitably camouflaged 108s flew as 109s in several films, perhaps most notably *The Longest Day*.

In *The Battle of Britain* some dozen 109s were assembled and were flown by pilots of the Confederate Air Force. These aircraft were Spanish-built (the Spanish built 109s immediately after the war and operated them up to the early 1960s). The sharp-eyed enthusiast will note that their Rolls-Royce Merlin engines gave them a nose profile different from the German Daimler-Benz engined 109s. In terms of movie glamour *The Battle of Britain* was the 109's finest hour.

During World War II the 109 was much filmed by the German propaganda ministry and when such footage eventually finds its way on to video it will be highly prized by enthusiasts.

1 THE SPITFIRE

Few names in British aviation history are quite so evocative as the Spitfire. In some strange way the name seems exactly appropriate for the machine. Moreover, it is synonymous with the Battle of Britain, with Churchill's 'Finest Hour' speech and with 'The Few' (echoing Shakespeare's 'Few – we happy few, we band of brothers' in *Henry V*). British history, oratory and literature are brought together in a little aeroplane as quintessentially British as a bowler hat.

The Spitfire pilot's life expectancy was short. According to Derek Wood and Derek Dempster in their classic book about the Battle of Britain, *The Narrow Margin* (Airlife, 1991) the life expectancy of a Battle of Britain fighter pilot was 87 (flying) hours:

Both air forces were bereaved of irreplaceable men, most of them in the flower of their youth. Counting pilots alone, Britain lost 415.

In contrast it is interesting to note that 451 pilots went through the whole of the battle and that 217 had been operational since the outbreak of war. The record for service goes to Flight Lieutenant J. C. Freeborn. He was posted to No 74 Squadron on October 29th 1938 and was still with the squadron at the end of November 1940. (p269)

The Spitfire legend is almost as old as the machine itself. Reginald J. Mitchell, the designer of the Spitfire, is the 'right stuff' of British heroism – a shy, quiet boffin battling with terminal illness whilst attempting to save Britain from the Nazi scourge with his wonder plane. *Boys' Own* stuff – but, in this case, true.

Such a good story could not be overlooked and the 1942 film *The First of the Few* (see page 12), appearing as it did just after the Battle of Britain, set the seal on the Spitfire legend. Although there were many more Hurricanes than Spitfires in 1940, it was the Spitfire which was promoted in the Ministry of Information propaganda. Unlike the Hurricane, which had reached its

technological limit, the Spitfire went on being improved, together with its naval derivative the Seafire, until well after the end of the war. It is remarkable that a 1936 aeroplane could still fly and fight on equal terms with the best piston-engined fighters at the end of the war.

This steady development resulted in numerous different 'marks', usually denoted by Roman numerals, and members of the Spitfire 'family' were employed in combat and/or photo reconnaissance roles in just about every theatre of operations during World War II – in North Africa with General Montgomery's Eighth Army (the Desert Rats), over the Normandy beaches in 1944, in the Far East, on aircraft carriers with the Royal Navy and finally in the victory parade fly-past. Just about every British, Allied and German soldier, sailor and civilian had seen a Spitfire (or Seafire, as the Fleet Air Arm Spitfires were known) by 1945.

The legend lived on; a Spitfire (and a Hurricane) led the Remembrance Day parade in London for decades after the war. Eventually the Royal Air Force Battle of Britain Memorial Flight was formed – including several Spitfires – which is active to this day. There is no reason why Spitfires should not fly regularly at air displays well into the twenty-first century, and hopefully at least one will fly in 2040 to commemorate the centenary of the Battle of Britain.

The admiration and affection shown by the public towards the Spitfire was shared in equal measure by RAF pilots, especially those who had actually flown the aircraft. Its superb handling, speed, rate of climb and the structural strength that enabled it to survive battle damage have become legendary. Several Spitfire pilots wrote memoirs lauding its virtues. During the war the Ministry of Information made a film featuring test pilot Alex Henshaw in which he puts the aircraft through a breathtaking display of aerobatics equal to the best seen at any air show today. When Goering asked his ace pilot Adolf Galland what he would like for his staff he replied 'a squadron of Spitfires'. The books written by Spitfire

pilots help to reinforce the legend, for by reading them we too are instantly transported into the cockpit. In addition there are endless numbers of books on the Spitfire, and of course on the art inspired by the plane.

The appeal of the Spitfire is enormous. The shape of the aircraft is exquisite, like some perfect, graceful animal. The curves are reminiscent of a big cat and similarly suggest power and strength.

The fact that its shape consists of compound curves is a feature especially challenging for the artist. The wings are elliptical and thin, the key to the aircraft's success. The fuselage is slender and beautifully proportioned, with the engine sleekly cowled. Even the drag-producing radiators are neatly tucked under the wings to leave a clean nose profile.

The Rolls-Royce Merlin engine gives the Spitfire marks their wonderful sound. Unlike modern jets, big piston aero engines emit a variety of sounds – starting up, ticking over, revving up, taxiing, taking off, climbing, diving, circling, coming in to land – indeed, enthusiasts buy recordings of Spitfires with tracks thus labelled.

The Spitfire is the most famous British aircraft of all time. Many other aircraft have come and gone in the years following World War II, but the Spitfire's popularity remains strong, rendered more attractive still by technological progress. Youngsters still build model Spitfires, and no doubt their children will after them. The Spitfire continues to be featured on book covers, on air display posters, and of course in the work of aviation artists.

The pictures that follow illustrate how this wonderful aircraft, possessed as it is of such timeless beauty, has caught the imagination of artists. Many choose to portray the aircraft in ways which show off its superb elliptical wings or its elegant streamlined fuselage. However artists portray it, the Spitfire always catches the eye and fires the imagination. It has that property of always looking wonderful however depicted and, when painted by artists of very great talent as in the following pages, looks just stunning.

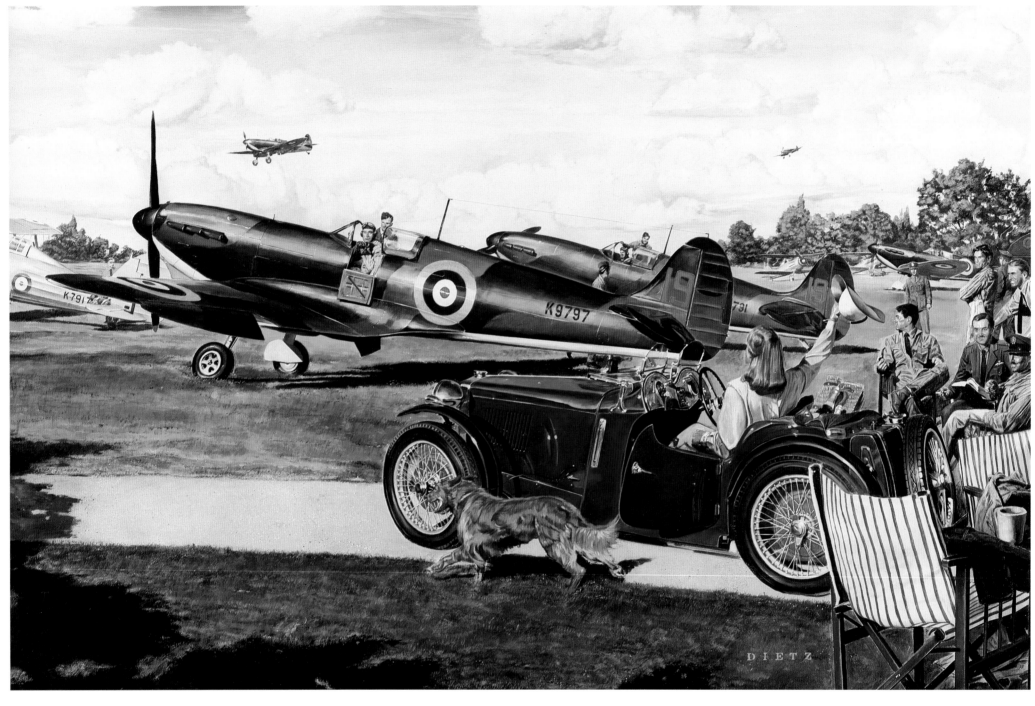

NEW KITES *Jim Dietz*
24 × 36in (61 × 91.5cm), oil.

Painting this picture must have been especially enjoyable for Jim Dietz, who is both a classic aircraft enthusiast and a keen appreciator of British pre-war sports cars, MGs in particular. The scene depicted shows the first Spitfires to enter service with the RAF during 1938. These are very early Mk Is with wooden fixed-pitch two-bladed propellers and are painted in pre-war markings with their squadron number on the fin in place of the later red white and blue

tricolour. It was said at the time that the RAF was the best flying club in the world! Certainly in this picture the artist has recreated that feeling of summer afternoon cricket-match rural idyll.

This scene is wistful and poignant – an image of innocence from a time before missiles and nuclear weapons. These heroes hail from an age as distant as Kipling's Raj, where more than a handful were born and grew up. Like the Raj, their world was doomed and by 1945 many of the pilots of 1938 had in the RAF slang of the time, 'bought it', 'got the chop' or 'gone for a Burton'.

However, in this frozen instant caught on canvas, the 'popsie' in the car waves eternally to her hero as he unstraps from his Spitfire, casually turning to smile as he does so. The faithful gun-dog runs from the car to greet his master as two 'Spits' lazily glide in to land. These are powerful images that go to the core of the British identity and also inflame the aeronautical (and motoring) enthusiast's passions.

In short, this is a lovely picture which draws us deep into itself in a reverie of imagination. The artist has managed to combine many elements to create a timeless scene.

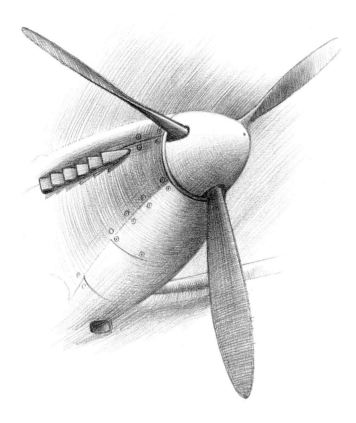

SPITFIRE NOSE
Vic McLindon

SPITFIRE *Geoffrey Lea*
20 × 16in (51 × 40.5cm), oil.

Fighter planes are always at their most dramatic in climbing or diving turns and this painting exploits this to the full. The artist has a very distinctive style, characterised by soft, warm, muted colours and an overall subtlety with the use of light. This is itself a reflection – artistically speaking – of the British climate, where bright, harsh sunlight is rare. Even the aircraft itself is rendered in a similarly gentle and soft-toned style.

For the enthusiastic eye there is, however, scrupulous attention to detail and technical accuracy. The overall effect is most attractive.

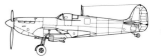

A MOMENT'S PEACE *Craig Kodera*
18 × 24in (45.5 × 61cm), oil on canvas.

This very striking painting is eye-catching by virtue of its predominant use of one colour. Sunlight and clouds produce some wonderful effects in nature, and artists have long sought to capture these; none more so than the aviation artist.

The composition of this painting is interesting in that the sun itself is the vanishing point and the two aircraft are perfectly positioned to complete the triangular composition. The perspective is further heightened by the nearer aircraft being positioned lower on the canvas than the second one, thereby also showing the lovely elliptical shape of the wings to greater effect.

It is interesting to note how the same type of aircraft in identical colour schemes can look so vastly different in varying lighting and cloudscapes. Compare this picture with Geoffrey Lea's 'Spitfire', for example, to see this point very well illustrated. These aircraft are two from Biggen Hill, flying during the Battle of Britain.

'JOHNNIE' JOHNSON'S SPITFIRE
Mark Postlethwaite
30 × 20in (76 × 51cm), acrylic on canvas.

This very dramatic picture is also notable for being of 'portrait' (ie upright) format rather than 'landscape'. This aspect of its composition greatly adds to the feeling of depth and dramatic action. The actual pose of the aircraft is also very dramatic, being part of an aerobatic manoeuvre.

The white streaks coming from the wing-tips are not merely added to suggest speed. Under high-speed 'g' loading this effect occurs naturally, the air vortex created at each wing-tip producing condensed water vapour in the atmosphere. It is physics' own artistic effect.

The lovely dark billowing cumulus clouds, so typical of the British Isles, provide a magnificent backdrop. They also serve to divide the canvas diagonally between lower right and upper left areas, the latter being blue sky. Postlethwaite has been careful to ensure that there is light cloud in just the right place to set off the superb contours of the Spitfire's wings to maximum effect. Similarly, the nose of the aircraft is sharply silhouetted against the clear blue sky behind.

This work has all the qualities of a 'pilot's picture' – it appeals to all those elements of excitement and pleasure that draw people to aircraft, both to fly them and to watch them being flown. It is also a celebration of the joy and freedom that is to be had at the controls of an aircraft like this, high in the sunlit silence.

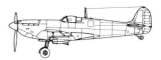
IMMORTAL HERO *David Shepherd*
30 × 36in (76 × 91.5cm), oil.

In this hauntingly beautiful picture David Shepherd has captured both the timeless beauty of the Spitfire and the feeling of vast space experienced when flying alone among cumulus clouds.

The Spitfire is perfectly posed to show off its wonderful elliptical wing planform and slender fuselage, itself moulded closely to the engine and thence smoothed into an oval and tapered to the tail. Poised trophy-like almost on the dark pinnacle of a cloud mountain, the aircraft seems immortal; frozen for an instant in space and time by the artist as an object of wonder for generations to come.

The shafts of bright sunlight coming directly from the top left corner of the picture highlight the fuselage and glint off canopy, cannon-barrels and exhausts. By highlighting one side of the fuselage the artist creates a feeling of depth and avoids the flat, dull effect so easily produced by lack of contrast or too even a source of light.

Movement is created by having the aircraft bank slightly to our right, nicely complementing the beams of sunlight striking it from the left. As we are viewing the aircraft from above and ahead, our brain tells us that, because the only external reference is cloud and there is no visible horizon or land, the aircraft must be cruising more or less horizontally. However, the combination of sunbeams, banking, and altitude creates a feeling of movement.

The colours of the camouflage pattern are reflected in the tremendous range of colour in both cloud and sunlight. Together a most effective result is produced. This is a very good example of a painting which at first glance may appear to have been very simply composed, but on closer examination is found to contain a complex and subtle blend of composition, perspective and colour, all used with great flair.

EAGLES' REST *Ronald Wong*
18 × 27in (45.5 × 69cm), oil.

Before the USA entered World War II American Pilots manned the famous Eagle Squadron of the RAF. Later, when the USAAF arrived in Britain, some Spitfires were made available to them, hence the American markings. Spitfires in American livery seem at first glance unusual, but this is an aspect of the history of this aircraft that should not be forgotten.

The rainbow in the distance brings to mind Judy Garland's 'Somewhere Over the Rainbow' from *The Wizard of Oz*, which was a very popular song during the war. Not surprisingly, the mid-1940s were characterised by a deep yearning for peace and the dawn of a new and better tomorrow. Thus, although a modern-day painting, this picture captures extremely well in an almost symbolic way, that wartime yearning for peace and a new beginning at the end of the rainbow.

Another element in this picture, frequently picked up by aviation artists, is the irresistible fascination of flight.

Individuals in scenes such as this nearly always stop to watch the aircraft fly by. This is not mere artistic licence but an accurate portrayal of human behaviour. By posing the two airmen on the Spitfire as he has done, Wong creates the impression that the aircraft is also casually at rest. The two in flight are in their element, whereas those on the ground stand silent and motionless.

The striking use of strong blue tones is characteristic of Ronald Wong's style and he uses water reflections in a most interesting way. Wet tarmac is certainly a very common feature of British airfields! The seemingly random scattering of bikes, oil-drums, a starter trolley and parked aircraft gives the composition good balance and additionally helps to frame the main subject. This is also true of the reflections of the two airmen in the water below the aircraft.

We are left to ponder where the two flying Spitfires are going and what will be their fate. Clearly they are not flying over the rainbow, but under it, and are on their way to a far harsher reality than Oz.

YANKS *Ronald Wong*
21 × 28in (53.5 × 71cm), oil.

American markings on a Spitfire may seem unusual to a British eye, but a number were flown by the US Army Air Forces during World War II. This classic study of a pair flying in close formation is a most pleasing picture, notable in a number of ways. The land is a study of various shades of blue with a reddened horizon line of late evening. The aircraft themselves, however, are in their correct colour tones and set off against the unusual light and background seem to emerge from the canvas. The artist has put a great deal of detail into the aircraft: even rivets and fasteners are clearly visible. The pilot of the nearest aircraft looks toward us from inside the cockpit, which glints as it reflects the light.

A notable feature of this painting is its style. Though a straightforward classic study of two Spitfires Ronald Wong's distinctive style, which he brings to all his paintings, marks it out from many similar pictures.

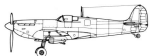

A FOGGY DAY *Charles J. Thompson*
24 × 36in (61 × 91.5cm), oil.

This painting shows off to perfection the superb lines of the Spitfire and in particular its elliptical wings. Charles Thompson uses several techniques of composition and colour to create a feeling of movement and interest in what might otherwise be a mere illustration.

Viewing the aircraft from this angle against patchy fog and cloud could indicate that the direction of flight is straight and level, but the angle of the River Thames relative to the aircraft's wings tells us instantly that it is turning towards us. The pilot in his cockpit looking in our direction enhances this feeling.

The cloud background changes from light to dark across the picture, so creating a sense of depth. Additionally the dividing line between dark and light cloud perfectly counters the axis of the wings and cuts through the centre of the fuselage.

The principal source of light reflects off the front flat panel of the cockpit but leaves the side panels next to it dark. This gives us a very clear signal as to the exact angle of the light but in addition helps to reinforce the idea that the aircraft is turning, for there is an instant when a turning aircraft's cockpit reflects light in just this way.

The propeller is of note as the artist has depicted it as a blue-tinged blur with a hint of yellow tip-streak. He has narrowed the yellow streak as it passes over the nose of the aircraft, which is geometrically correct, and indicates meticulous attention to detail.

This is a most delightful study, which illustrates well how the seemingly simple often proves to be far more subtle and complex on closer examination.

25

TOP COVER *Frank Wootton*
25 × 36in (63.5 × 91.5cm), oil.

The best place to have a fighter escort is above the bombers where it can dive down on to an attacking enemy. This fine study emphasises the protective role of the fighter planes very well.

Because of the perspective the bomber formation is apparently under the wings of the lead Spitfire. Again because of the perspective, the Spitfire appears very large while the bombers are tiny and, by implication, vulnerable.

The two formations reflect each other in terms of artistic composition, both groups forming a triangle.

The use of cloud helps to set off the two Spitfires in the background and also, by running from bottom left to centre top, harmonises with the left side of the triangle created by the Spitfire formation. The coastline runs parallel with the fuselage of the lead Spitfire and the bombers' line of flight. This is partly a compositional decision, but perhaps also not unconnected with air navigation at that time.

Once again we are drawn into the picture by the Spitfire pilot's glance in our direction as if we too are part of this formation. There is plenty of fine detail, for instance we can see that the pilot's goggles are pushed up on his forehead.

The lovely blues, cloud formation and barren landscape provide a dramatic and bright setting for the aircraft portrayed in this picture – a skyscape familiar to many holidaymakers who fly to sunny climes. Once more, though, the Spitfire is the star and its wonderful lines, so beautifully caught here, will always delight those who love aircraft.

FIRST OF THE MANY *Michael Turner*
20 × 16in (51 × 40.5cm), gouache.

'Oohs' and 'Aahs' are frequently heard at air shows whenever there is a good aerobatic display. This picture of a Spitfire flown by test pilot Alex Henshaw at Castle Bromwich, Birmingham, perfectly captures that instant of intense excitement and pleasure provided by a fine aircraft flown by a skilled pilot. It is especially eye-catching and dramatic for several reasons.

The aircraft is depicted in a very unusual and exciting attitude: at the top of a rolling vertical climb. It is trailing wing-tip condensation vortices – a sign of high-speed and high-'g' flight. We are viewing the aircraft from an aerial vantage point such that the horizon is tilted. This creates a feeling of the Spitfire rolling as it climbs vertically so that we too feel that we are in the manoeuvring aircraft.

There is a tremendous depth in this picture – almost a 3-D effect – produced by a combination of soft haze in the background and fine detail in the foreground. It is quite easy to count individual aircraft and houses on the ground, for example.

But it is the main subject that commands our attention, the sheer beauty of the Spitfire with its delightful elliptical wing a joy to behold.

'This painting, which was presented to the City of Birmingham, depicts one of the first machines to be produced at the Castle Bromwich airfield.

In June 1940 ten aircraft were built almost in desperation as Britain faced invasion. When production reached 320 aircraft each month the Castle Bromwich factory became the showpiece of the British aircraft industry at war.

High-ranking missions came from Allied and neutral countries. In order to demonstrate convincingly the Spitfire's superiority over comparable enemy fighters, my job was to fly an aerobatic sequence far beyond what might be expected from a first-line fighter aircraft.

This painting portrays the completion of three upward vertical rolls starting from near ground level after a dive to nearly 500mph and which formed part of a demanding display that would leave no doubt in the minds of US and Soviet aviation experts that this was a fighting machine of unchallengeable supremacy.'

ALEX HENSHAW

DEADLY CHASE *Ronald Wong*
18 × 27in (45.5 × 69cm), oil.

The closing phases of World War II were marked by the appearance of a radical new technology. In particular jet aircraft, missiles and liquid-fuelled rockets were used for the first time in anger. In this most dramatic and striking picture Ronald Wong has achieved two things: the feeling of tremendous speed and the clash of old and new technologies.

The feeling of extremely rapid flight is produced by the blurred background and, a slightly less obvious point, its

distance from the aircraft. This is not 'on the deck' speed where a hundred miles an hour can seem like a thousand. In addition, the blur continues right out to the horizon, several miles away. The Spitfire and the V-1 are both in a gentle turn, another device which creates a feeling of dynamism in the picture.

The novelty of the picture is outstanding: a Spitfire chasing a flying bomb! The aircraft is closing in on the V-1 'Doodle Bug' intending to force up its wing with its own wing tip, thereby causing the V-1 to go out of control and crash into the ground before reaching its target.

The V-1, predecessor to the cruise missile, still looks modern even though in reality it was no more than a

winged bomb with a pulse jet and a simple gyro auto-pilot for guidance. However, being essentially a jet aircraft, the V-1 pointed to the propellerless future. Though a subsonic missile, its nose contours suggest supersonic flight unlike the propeller-driven Spitfire.

The artist has created much more than an image; he has created a piece of art which stirs our thinking, forcing us to remake old connections or create new thoughts and ideas. He has portrayed that instant when man's conquest of the air entered new territory. That is reason enough to make this a most remarkable picture, but when combined with the wonderful effect of speed and drama which he has produced the overall result is outstanding.

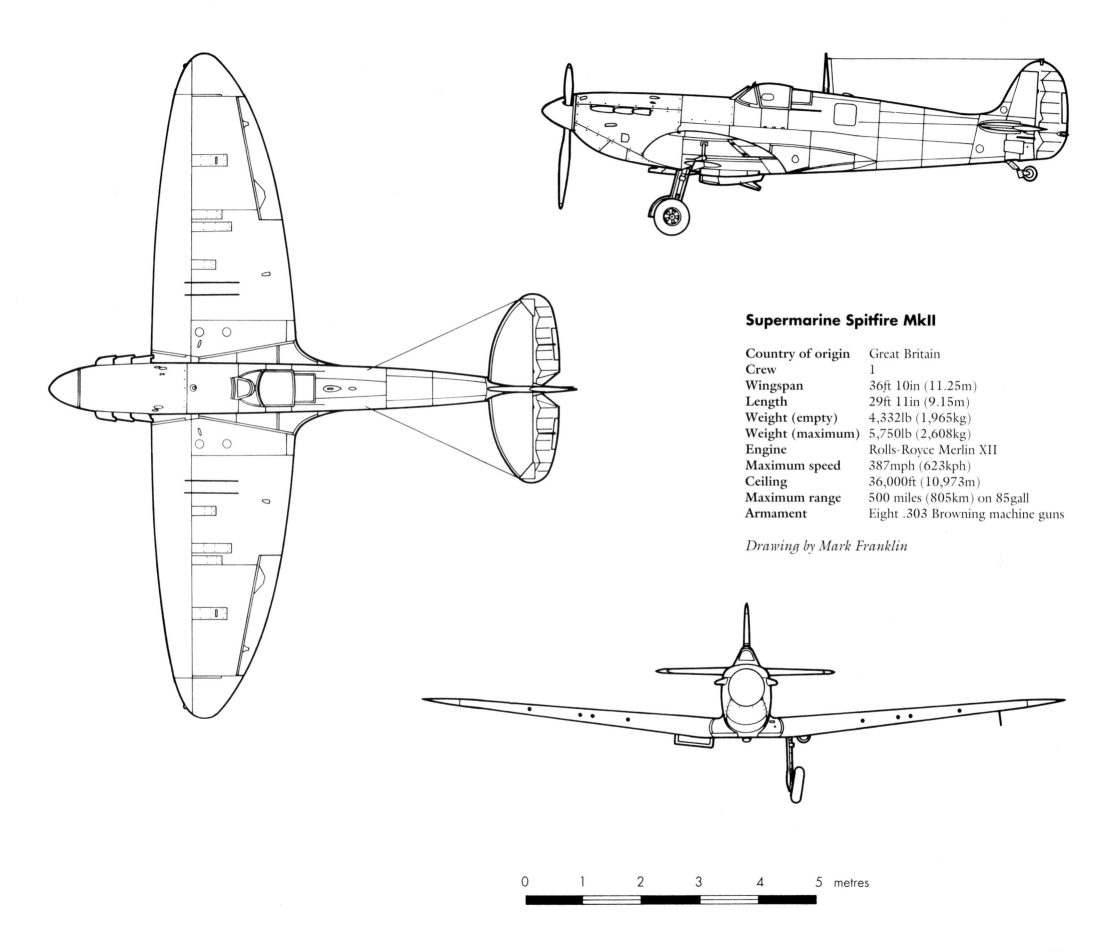

Supermarine Spitfire MkII

Country of origin	Great Britain
Crew	1
Wingspan	36ft 10in (11.25m)
Length	29ft 11in (9.15m)
Weight (empty)	4,332lb (1,965kg)
Weight (maximum)	5,750lb (2,608kg)
Engine	Rolls-Royce Merlin XII
Maximum speed	387mph (623kph)
Ceiling	36,000ft (10,973m)
Maximum range	500 miles (805km) on 85gall
Armament	Eight .303 Browning machine guns

Drawing by Mark Franklin

0   1   2   3   4   5   metres

2 THE LANCASTER

'Right a bit . . . steady . . . left . . . steady . . . steady . . . bombs gone!'
Those words have often been heard on the soundtracks of films about Bomber Command. They conjure up images of flak, probing searchlights and gunfire from 'tail-end charlie' which characterised the Lancasters' frequent raids over Hitler's Germany.

Of all the thousands of missions flown, one single exploit is indelibly connected with the Lancaster – the Dam Busters raid. First recorded in a book of that name by Paul Brickhill, and later presented as a film starring

LANCASTER WIRELESS OPERATOR
Anthony Saunders

Richard Todd as Guy Gibson, the event is now as much a part of British history as the Battle of Trafalgar or the Charge of the Light Brigade. Just as their forebears had ridden into the valley of death so too did these airmen fly up the Möhne and Eder valleys with flak thundering and volleying at them.

Unlike the Light Brigade, however, the Dam Busters of 617 Squadron were thoroughly briefed. It was no accident of fate that brought them to that place at that moment in history: science and engineering combined to make it happen. Only specially modified Lancasters were capable of carrying the famous cylindrical 'bouncing bomb', brainchild of Barnes Wallis, to the Ruhr dams. Thus was the legend born.

The Lancaster, like the Spitfire, has a pedigree that reaches back to the 1930s. Originally conceived as a twin-engined aircraft, when it was named the Manchester, it was unsuccessful because of the unreliability of its two Rolls-Royce Vulture engines. Roy Chadwick, the aircraft's brilliant designer, plucked success from the jaws of failure by lengthening the wings and installing four Rolls-Royce Merlins in place of the two Vultures. The rest, as they say, is history.

Part of the Lancaster legend relates to its immense structural strength. Time after time, Lancasters returned home with huge holes in various parts of the structure and on half power. Some even made it back to base on one engine. This strength derived from the fact that the Manchester had been designed to withstand catapult-assisted take-off with heavy bomb loads from short runways. The fuselage accordingly had two massive beams in its lower structure running the length of the fuselage and these enabled enormous bomb loads to be carried without the need for extra strengthening.

The Lancaster was a great aeroplane in every possible respect, including performance, serviceability and handling characteristics. Its flying controls were particularly well harmonised and the stick loads were agreeably low, making the aircraft responsive and easy to fly. Many men owe their lives to its outstanding qualities. One post-war

development, the Shackleton, continued in RAF service until 1991.

If the appeal of an aircraft like the Spitfire lies in its sheer beauty, the appeal of the Lancaster is in its impressiveness. It still seems huge even in an age of jumbo jets. Four Merlin engines create an immensely powerful sound, even though all four together produce less power than any one on most modern jet airliners.

Despite its size, the Lancaster is still aesthetically pleasing. The fuselage is beautifully slender with the three gun turrets very neatly designed to produce minimum drag. The cockpit canopy sits atop the fuselage fighter-style, giving a panoramic view (this at a time when stepped fuselage cockpits were common – as on the Halifax for example). The twin fins and rudders are beautiful elliptical shapes reminiscent of shields. The overall impression is of a very neat, clean, harmonious design, – and somehow the whole seems to be more than the sum of its parts. It is an aircraft that 'looks right'.

In its Bomber Command wartime colour scheme, the Battle of Britain Memorial Flight Lancaster is one of only two still flying at the time of writing. A frequent visitor to air displays, it brings to each generation the thrill of seeing one of these magnificent machines in all its glory. There is no reason why this marvellous aircraft should not continue to fly well into the twenty-first century, a piece of living history to delight and enthral future generations.

Books such as Guy Gibson's *Enemy Coast Ahead*, Leonard Cheshire's *Bomber Pilot* and, of course, Paul Brickhill's *The Dam Busters* will ensure that the legend lives on. Generations of youngsters will build models of the Lancaster just as they have since it was developed. In a well-known photograph taken in 1944 of Roy Chadwick with an air cadet, Chadwick is examining the boy's model Lancaster with the totally absorbed eye of the engineer while the boy looks up at his hero with awe.

With such a distinguished pedigree, classic design and legendary history it is no surprise that the Lancaster has been the subject of an enormous amount of British aeronautical art. Many artists still receive commissions to paint Lancasters – in specific markings as flown by individuals; to show off the tail turret where a veteran flew and fought; or on the ground being serviced and bombed-up for an op. The following exciting paintings depict the Lancaster in a wide variety of poses that set off its many facets to full advantage.

BOMBING-UP A 'LANC'
Vic McLindon
Impressive still, awesome then, the mighty Lancaster's cavernous bomb-bay is loaded with tons of bombs.

ROY CHADWICK, LANCASTER DESIGNER
Geoffrey Lea
20 × 30in (51 × 76cm), oil.

Aircraft designers are often unsung heroes. Roy Chadwick was one such whose career began with Edwardian biplanes at the very dawn of flight and ended with the mighty Vulcan jet bomber. In this fine portrait he is shown in the pilot's seat of his most famous design, the Avro Lancaster bomber.

Although a qualified pilot, he gave up testing his own designs in 1920 following a severe crash caused by freezing conditions. Thereafter he always flew with Avro test pilots. He was one of the last of the 'slide-rule' engineers and could carry huge amounts of information in his head. He frequently toured the design office and workshops, discussing minute details with individual engineers and workers. Originally a machine-shop apprentice, when he became a top designer he was never above donning overalls, clambering aboard an aircraft and sorting out problems at first hand. After its initial engine problems were rectified, the Lancaster went on to become the mainstay of RAF Bomber Command.

Chadwick received many honours in his lifetime, including the CBE for designing the Lancaster following the famous Dam Busters raid by 617 Squadron in 1943. He died prematurely and tragically in 1947 at the age of 54 when an aircraft in which he was flying crashed due to the controls having been wrongly connected.

I have been privileged to meet a great many people who knew Roy Chadwick well, including his surviving family. Not only was he a totally dedicated aero engineer with a deep love of aircraft but he was also a very kind and considerate man, liked and respected by all who knew him. These qualities have been well caught by Geoffrey Lea in this fine study.

LANCASTER TOUCHDOWN *Frank Munger*
11 × 18in (28 × 45.5cm), watercolour.

Frank Munger specialises in watercolours and usually paints very early aircraft. This picture is an exception to the latter rule. During the war he served some time on Wellington squadrons and saw many scenes such as this daily – although of course the subject of this painting is a Lancaster.

Watercolour work has a delightful, almost transparent, delicacy and in this picture the medium lends itself admirably to a snow scene. The big black aircraft contrasts sharply with the greys of the snow and slush. The surface water on the runway reflects the wheels and picks up hints of blue from the sky. The cloud and light-ray patterns in the sky enhance the perspective and, combined with the aircraft's very slight right-wing-down attitude, help create a feeling of movement. The snow tracks in the foreground echo and reinforce this element.

This is further accentuated by the stillness of the figures who have stopped to watch the landing. Even, perhaps especially, those who work with aircraft find the sight of aircraft landing irresistible and the airman on the bicycle is watching with rapt attention.

This is a picture of wonderful light delicacy, full of feeling for the subject and, by virtue of its medium and style, sadly a rarity in aviation art.

'I started to paint using watercolour in the late 1940s, so it was natural that when I later started to do aviation subjects I should use that medium. Although I later came to paint in other media I have always found watercolour suits the way I see aeroplanes and their environment, particularly skies, which I think are the key to a painting – setting both the mood and atmosphere. I seem to have acquired some sort of name for delicate watercolours of aviation subjects, but I still think there are some settings for which oil (or acrylic) is more suitable.

I enjoy the spontaneity of watercolour and the speed with which one can attain a result. I find it is most suitable in portraying the lightness and delicacy of early aircraft.'

FRANK MUNGER

'I find the Lancaster one of the most pleasing of the big bombers to paint. The concentration of glass around the front end stealing every glimmer of light from every angle creating a dramatic cascade of reflected light from any front view. The beautiful shape of the wing with its pronounced dihedral from the inner engines gives one the impression that it could, at any moment, start flapping (as indeed they did if viewed from on board during turbulence!).'

ROBIN SMITH

LANCASTER STUDY *Robin Smith*
20 × 24in (51 × 61cm), oil.

This lovely painting shows to great advantage the beautiful wing shape of the aircraft which did so much to give it its outstanding performance. The clouds help to silhouette the shape of the whole aircraft and make it stand out. The dark nose and black propeller spinners create an animal-like 'face' making the machine seem almost alive. Certainly the life of this beast, its vibrant energy and power generated by four huge piston engines, comes across to us.

We can readily imagine what it must have been like for the crew seated behind those glazed panels. Noisy and cramped perhaps, but also uniquely exhilarating.

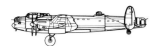

LANCASTER FORMATION *Frank Wootton*
25 × 36in (63.5 × 91.5cm), oil.

Frank Wootton was one of the earliest exponents of British aviation art. As such, he is in the rare position of being able to draw on actual memories of wartime aircraft.

This handsome study of a Lancaster is very striking and is enhanced by the dramatic clouds which are billowing up like Alpine landscapes. It is interesting to note how he has used reflected light on the propeller spinners to great effect as well as highlighting the canopy and nose. The flickering glow from the exhausts has also been highlighted. This is a detail often missed in pictures of Lancasters. Although covers were fitted to obscure the exhaust glow, this was sometimes the giveaway light that was spotted by prowling enemy night fighters.

LANCASTERS RETURN AT DAWN *Michael Turner*
16 × 24in (40.5 × 61cm), gouache.

It was often said at the time that the greatest sound for any Lancaster crew was that made by the wheels touching down at the end of a mission. This picture beautifully captures that moment.

In the foreground we have a fine study of a Lancaster.

The aircraft looks as if it has been on many missions as its paint is scratched and worn and there are oil and smoke stains on its cowlings and wings. Clearly a good old 'kite' that can be relied on to bring its crew back again and again. (It is a fact that crews often refused new aircraft, preferring an old dependable 'Lanc' to an unknown if factory-fresh replacement.)

The lines of the aircraft draw our eyes to the Lancaster

with the burning engine. Its zig-zag smoke trail suggests a bumpy landing – perhaps its control surfaces are damaged or the pilot wounded. Beyond, other aircraft are on final approach to the aerodrome and a Very light arcs across the sky in which dawn is breaking.

This is a painting that one can lose oneself in. An especially fine work.

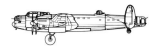

ALEX HENSHAW'S LANCASTER FLIGHT TEST
Michael Turner
20 ×14in (51 × 35.5cm), gouache.

Many times, and by many pilots, flying has been described as 'hours of boredom punctuated by moments of stark terror'. This is such a moment.

Alex Henshaw is a famous test pilot who flew many aircraft of this period including the Lancaster. The event depicted actually occurred when the dinghy came adrift and wrapped itself around the tail of the aircraft with the result shown in the painting! At the time ejector seats were not available, so in the ensuing moments the pilot had the choice of attempting to bail out – more or less impossible given the aircraft's speed and angle of dive – or stay with it. Happily for both Alex and posterity (he went on to write a fascinating book of memoirs – *Sigh for a Merlin*) the dinghy broke free in the nick of time and he managed to regain control with only feet to spare. It is not known what speed the aircraft reached or how many 'g' were pulled during the recovery from the dive, but it is certain that Alex also owed his life to Roy Chadwick, the designer of this fabulous and unbelievably strong aeroplane.

'This machine was completing a full-power dive on a production test-flight when the dinghy was forced out of the starboard wing and became entangled over the tailplane and elevators. This pitched the aircraft into a much steeper uncontrollable situation that threatened to scatter both machine and crew over the vast industrial city below.

I shouted into the intercom for my flight-test crew to bail out and I struggled with the machine as it plunged earthwards at over 400mph. As I grappled hopelessly with the controls, my impression was that the wings would be torn off even before we hit the ground. (The Lancaster, in any case, was somewhat longitudinally unstable at speeds in excess of 360mph. Extremely careful handling of the elevator trimming tabs was necessary to check excessive stick-control loads.)

I struggled in desperation, shouting all the time for the crew to jump. Either the shrieking noise and violent buffeting might have frozen them to their posts or perhaps in the confusion they simply failed to comprehend the order. I could not give up wrestling with the controls until I was sure my crew had jumped, and in those last split seconds prepared myself mentally for the worst. Suddenly, with a violent shudder and lurch, I felt the dinghy break away and I pulled the machine up over the house and factory roofs with precious little height to spare.'

ALEX HENSHAW

DAMBUSTERS *Robert Taylor*
28 × 40in (71 × 101.5cm), oil on canvas.

Robert Taylor's dramatic picture captures the moment when 'Mick' (later Air Marshal Sir Harold) Martin's Lancaster P 'Popsie' releases the Barnes Wallis bouncing bomb on its successful bombing run up to the Möhne Dam. Above and to the right is Guy Gibson, commanding officer of 617 Squadron, gallantly drawing enemy fire away from Martin.

The inferno of the dam lies ahead; the principal source of light in the picture comes from the effects of the bomb dropped by John Hopgood, which bounced over the dam and struck the power station just beyond. In addition to this, Hopgood's aircraft crashed in flames a few miles beyond the power station.

The stream of tracer coming from the dam and passing under the left wing of P 'Popsie' serves to create a sense of speed and depth. This is an extremely effective device particularly in a picture which, by virtue of being a night scene over water, gives little indication of height or speed. This is not only a problem for artists but was a problem for the pilots involved in the raid – hence the use of the two vital height-indicating spotlights. It is also worth noting that the altitude of the attacking aircraft on this raid was less than the wingspan of the Lancaster itself!

Of all the actions fought with Lancasters during World War II, this one raid is perhaps the most outstanding. It has become a truly legendary part of aviation history, deservedly so as it combines gallantry of the highest order, inventive genius without parallel and one of the most outstanding aircraft of all time. In this exciting and dramatic picture Robert Taylor has captured one of the supreme moments of this mission in a way which draws us into the action and undoubtedly fires the imagination.

EVENING DEPARTURE *Gerald Coulson*
24 × 36in (61 × 91.5cm), oil.

Even in this age of jumbo jets the Lancaster is still an extremely impressive aeroplane. The sight and sound of one taking off is memorable – in its day it must have been awesome!

In this painting Gerald Coulson has captured that feeling of size and power as all four Merlins, running flat out at 3,000rpm and 12lb of boost, strain to drag the heavily laden bomber into the evening air. The aircraft is mostly matt black – the standard wartime Bomber Command colour scheme – and the effect is to produce a near-silhouette against the clear sky and strato cumulus clouds. The rays of the setting sun dramatically catch the canopy, nose turret, tyres and radiators, which emphasises the dark, compact shape of the aeroplane.

The propellers are especially noteworthy in this picture as they so perfectly catch the light to create yellow-edged blurs (caused by the painted blade-tips) so typical of props on take-off. This effect is enhanced by the exhaust flames to produce that magnificent roar of power which this picture triggers in the viewer's imagination.

Churchill described the Spitfires as the shield and the Lancasters as the sword – the former Britain's salvation and the latter its source of victory. This is a fine study of that shining sword.

OUTWARD BOUND *Charles J. Thompson*
16 × 20in (40.5 × 51cm), oil.

This striking study of a Lancaster is notable for the
outstanding beauty of the skyscape and the viewpoint
chosen for the aircraft itself. Looking along the wings of
the Lancaster our eye is drawn to the sun, whose rays
frame the aircraft in a triangle of beams. This creates a
wonderful feeling of light and space whilst at the same

time setting off the aircraft in sharp relief. The clouds
themselves range in tone from dark to light in a radial
pattern centred on the sun, itself partially obscured by
cloud. The dark cloud in turn helps to mark out the profile
of the far wing tip.

Reflections coming from the water in the bottom part of
the picture balance the light in the upper area. In effect the
horizon line is created not at the horizon itself but at the
level of the sun along the top edge of the cloud base. The

artist's attention to detail is excellent, and the turret and
cockpit are meticulously reproduced.

This is a lovely study of the Lancaster, which is an
especially fine looking aeroplane. The use of colour and
light is reminiscent of Turner who, had he lived in the age
of flight, might perhaps have been tempted to paint
aeroplanes like this.

WINTER OF '43 SOMEWHERE IN ENGLAND
David Shepherd
24 × 44in (61 × 112cm), oil.

This well-known and lovely painting is a classic in aviation art; deservedly so, for many reasons.

The composition is extremely effective. It draws our eye straight to the aircraft which itself is posed to best effect showing off its huge wings and lovely nose contours that are the hallmark of the Lancaster. It is a picture with plenty of human interest; there is indeed a story being related. We can see that this mechanical war-bird requires the concerted teamwork of many to function. Its appetite for fuel, oil, bombs, ammunition and spares can only be sated by ground-crew teams supplied and equipped with all the best that the technology of the day could produce.

The bomber and its support equipment stand in stark contrast to the rural setting. Here in a field in a corner of England amidst the earth, grass, bare trees and open skies

stands this war machine crammed with miles of electrical wiring, radar and radio sets, filled with thousands of gallons of fuel and armed with tons of bombs. And yet, in this rural idyll more in keeping with cavalry and bowmen, this Lancaster also seems to be in its natural habitat when at rest. The entire scene becomes totally at one with nature.

> 'I painted this picture for the RAF Benevolent Fund, as a gesture of appreciation – it was the RAF in Nairobi who in 1960 commissioned my first wildlife painting. Prints of the painting raised a considerable sum for the Fund, and the project had the added benefit of enabling me to fly in PA474, City of Lincoln, the sole remaining Lancaster flying in Britain.'
>
> DAVID SHEPHERD

LONG NIGHT AHEAD *Gerald Coulson*
30 × 40in (76 × 101.5cm), oil.

Above the clouds which so often fill European skies the sun always shines. Gerald Coulson has a love of this above-the-clouds daylight setting and he has used it on several occasions; here to great effect. One can sense the bitter cold of the still air as the four-engined 'heavy', unseen yet heard from the ground, drones towards its night battle over the Reich.

Almost silhouetted against the cold blue sky, the bomber's fuselage and wing are caught by the rays of the fast-setting sun which pick out its every detail. Seen from this angle it almost appears to hover in the air like a kestrel hunting for its prey. Such is this kind of warfare, however, that the Lancaster itself may fall prey to the night fighters who, unseen and bat-like, stalk the night skies looking for the faint radar echoes of bombers such as this.

MISTS OF TIME *Geoffrey Lea*
30 × 48in (76 × 122cm), oil.

The Lincolnshire Fens are where many of the Lancaster bases were sited during the war. In this very atmospheric and evocative picture the artist has put the aircraft, perhaps symbolically, in both its natural elements: the air and the Lincolnshire landscape. Some would consider the idea of a machine having a 'natural' element to be pure romanticism, but for those who love aircraft and are irresistibly drawn to aviation art, and those too who perhaps remember the Lancaster in its heyday, a picture such as this is, and always will be, far more than a mere image of a machine. The Lancaster's size, shape, beauty and perhaps above all its history, convey many emotions. For some, such a picture can indeed bring a tear to the eye.

This is a very fine study of a classic aircraft and one that absorbs the viewer more deeply the longer it is viewed.

'This painting was a spin-off from my involvement to research and paint two portraits of Roy Chadwick, the designer of the Lancaster. (One of these is reproduced on page 31.) My admiration for the man and his outstanding genius led me to look again at the Lancaster. Because I now knew rather more about its origins, I saw it anew and could discern even more clearly what a truly wonderful machine this was.

In this painting I have tried to capture some of the feeling of nostalgia for the period. The actual mists of the Lincolnshire Fens also symbolise the mists of time. I chose this angle after much careful consideration of all possible angles from which to view the aircraft. It is surprising what an enormous difference can be made to a painting by moving the viewpoint even slightly. As I have it here, I feel that it is just right and that any alteration of the aircraft's position or angle would reduce the harmony of the study.

I favour soft, muted tones and autumnal scenes and this painting gave me an opportunity to develop this aspect of my style to the full.'

GEOFFREY LEA

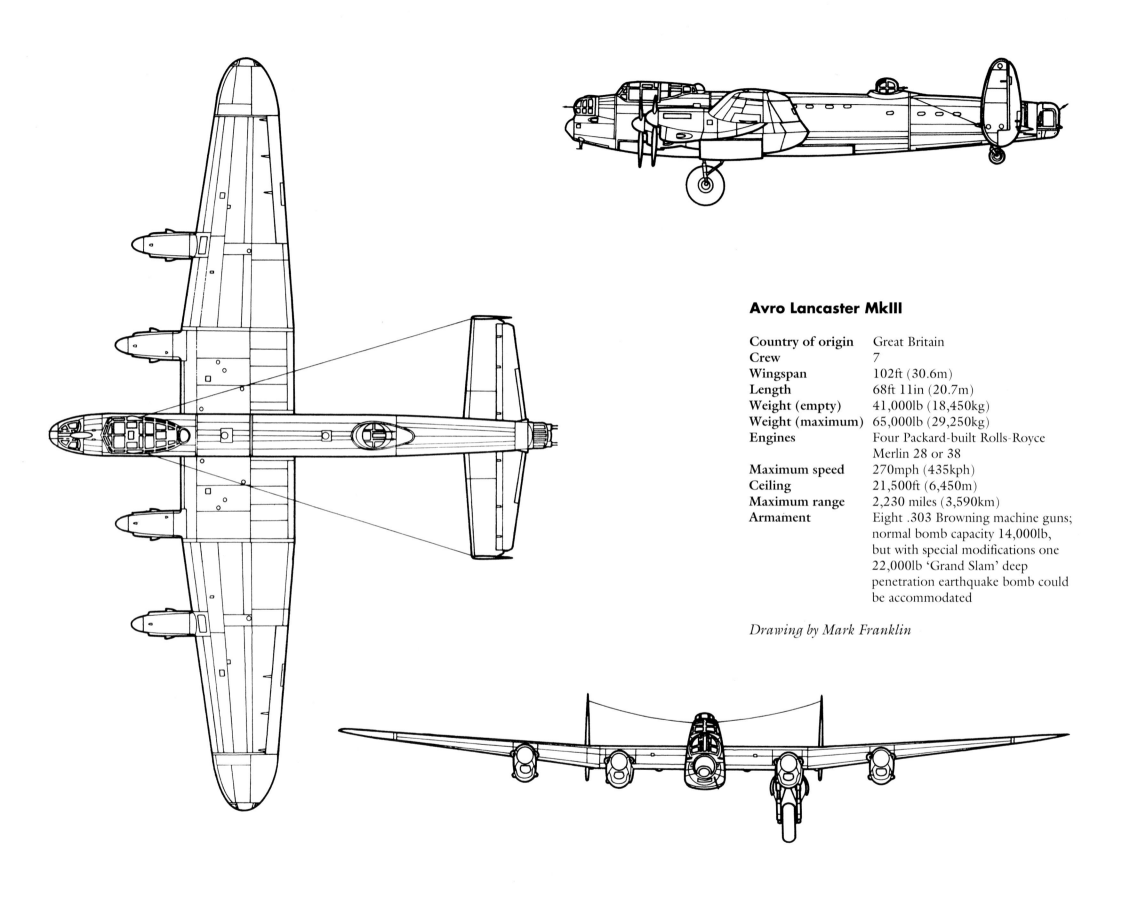

Avro Lancaster MkIII

Country of origin	Great Britain
Crew	7
Wingspan	102ft (30.6m)
Length	68ft 11in (20.7m)
Weight (empty)	41,000lb (18,450kg)
Weight (maximum)	65,000lb (29,250kg)
Engines	Four Packard-built Rolls-Royce Merlin 28 or 38
Maximum speed	270mph (435kph)
Ceiling	21,500ft (6,450m)
Maximum range	2,230 miles (3,590km)
Armament	Eight .303 Browning machine guns; normal bomb capacity 14,000lb, but with special modifications one 22,000lb 'Grand Slam' deep penetration earthquake bomb could be accommodated

Drawing by Mark Franklin

0 1 2 3 4 5 6 metres

3 THE BOEING B-17 FLYING FORTRESS

The movie cowboy and the modern American fighting man are inextricably intertwined in the popular imagination on both sides of the Atlantic. It is no coincidence that, after winning the congressional medal of honour, Audie Murphy went on to star in cowboy films.

It is against this backdrop that the B-17 can be understood. The aircraft is a twentieth-century metaphor for the frontier and is characterised by the same elements: plenty of firepower, sweeping through the skies in tight-knit squadrons like cavalry, defending democracy against the bad guys. Add to this the music of Glenn Miller, the sharp uniforms, jeeps and chewing gum and the result is a heady mixture of old and new. To the British at the time it must have seemed that Hollywood had suddenly come to England. In a way it had: film stars Jimmy Stewart and Clark Gable were flying with the Eighth Air Force!

'Flying Fortress' was never an official USAAF name, but a Boeing company name. Its crews simply called it a B-17. The name has great significance however. The words 'Flying Fortress' imply isolationism and aircraft like the B-17 were part of 'hemisphere defence' – an antique term now but in the 1940s totally familiar. The Fortress that was developed to fly in defence of American shores was originally just that – a long-range patrol bomber never intended for strategic bombing: hence its small bomb-bay and tiny bomb load, even by the standards of the day. For this reason the B-17s had to raid en masse to produce a worthwhile bombing offensive. And so it was.

The B-17 was inspired by the ideas of the early air strategists like Mitchell, Douhet and Seversky who believed in what became known in American military aviation circles as 'the ascendancy of bombardment over pursuit'. Simply put, this doctrine stated that bombers will always be superior to defensive fighters because they can tote plenty of flexibly mounted firepower and fly in tight self-defending formations. Moreover, because these strategists never foresaw radar, they thought fighter air

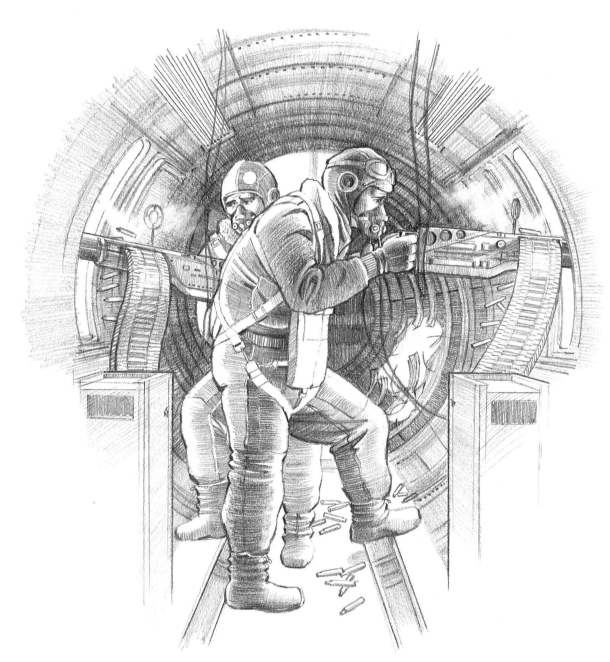

B-17 WAIST GUNNERS
Vic McLindon

44

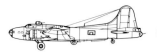

forces would need to be large enough to mount defensive patrols over each likely target whereas a bomber fleet need only be sufficiently large to destroy one major target. It was an elegantly simple and plausible theory, but disastrously wrong! Certainly bombing, both strategic (against war industry) and tactical (against communications and troop concentrations), does win wars, but 'the ascendancy of bombardment over pursuit' is, metaphorically, pie in the sky.

Dr Goebbels' propaganda ministry had a field day when B-17s began raiding Europe in daylight without fighter escorts. In western parlance, the first raids were aerial last stands in the Custer tradition. German newsreels showed dejected US airmen, crashing B-17s and jubilant Luftwaffe fighter pilots graphically recounting their kills. This time the Indians were as well armed as the cavalry. The early operations were disastrous. On the first raid with a force of nearly 400 aircraft, 60 were destroyed. On the second raid, with 287 aircraft, another 60 were lost – a total of 1200 men. To be successful, daylight bombing raids had to have fighter escort.

In spite of this, or perhaps because of it, the legend was born. In 1943 William Wyler made the all-time classic film *Memphis Belle* (see page 14), and Hollywood has periodically made B-17 movies ever since, recently completing the circle with a *Memphis Belle* remake.

What was there about this slice of aeronautical history that has so caught the public imagination? One element is undoubtedly the gunfight *per se*. In particular the waist-gunners (one each side in a B-17, both with a .50 calibre hand-aimed gun) have been most remembered. These gun positions were a unique feature of the B-17; the other positions in the aircraft had power-operated multi-gun turrets like those in the Lancaster. Obviously from a filming point of view the waist-gunners were the easiest to photograph and so most of the action featured them. A man blasting away at incoming fighters with a large hand-swung machine gun makes for some great footage. Many arcade video games are rehashes of this basic theme even if now the incoming 'bandits' are extraterrestrial. This image strikes a very deep chord and mankind's hunting instinct responds to it. If nothing else, B-17 raids were often protracted gunfights against both enemy fighters and anti-aircraft artillery.

The B-17 still seems a very large and impressive aeroplane. A few are still in flying condition and can be seen at air displays in Britain and the USA. To anyone who has seen one flying it is as memorable a sight and sound as any aircraft. First flown in the mid-1930s, the B-17 was at the time the most advanced large bomber in the world. In fact it was also the world's largest production warplane. It is hard for us to appreciate just what a futuristic revelation the B-17 was to the people of 1935 – a time when fabric-covered biplanes were still commonplace. The design was a triumph of elegant streamlining which set a standard that has survived virtually unchanged. The fuselage is of circular cross-section and tapers to a near-point with a slender fin and rudder. Later models have a deeper rear fuselage with a tail-gunner position and a much enlarged fin which extends along the back of the fuselage – a unique feature then, now much more commonplace. It looks every inch an American aeroplane: big, well designed, well built and heavily armed. While other air forces were thinking in terms of small tactical bombers, the United States Army Air Corps was literally thinking big. And this was the result.

Just as it is impossible to look at a Colt .45 and not think of the Wild West, so it is impossible to see a B-17 without thinking of the aerial shoot-out that was the Eighth Air Force's war against the Luftwaffe. The pictures that follow capture that feeling perfectly.

Note: The US Army Air Corps (formed in 1926) was subsequently given autonomous command within the Army and, on 20 June 1941, was renamed the US Army Air Forces (USAAF). On 26 July 1947 the name was again changed to the US Air Force (USAF).

B-17 WAIST GUNNER
Anthony Saunders

THE RETURN OF THE BELLE *Robert Taylor*
28 × 42in (71 × 107cm), oil on canvas.

Virtually every B-17 had a name and some form of 'nose art', usually of a comic or erotic nature. This aircraft, perhaps the most famous B-17 of all, was named after a lady destined to become the wife of the aircraft's Captain and pilot, Colonel Robert Morgan.

The painting has a wonderful golden tone so redolent of the 'Constable country' where most B-17s were based – the Essex and Suffolk counties of England. This is a scene which we can all be readily drawn into, the narrow English lane running beside the airfield boundary where grandstand views of landing aircraft swooping overhead at treetop height could be readily and frequently seen. The two men and their dog are of one world; the *Belle* of another. A couple of hours earlier the aircraft may have been involved in a running battle with Luftwaffe fighters at 30,000 feet. It may even have some battle-scars from flak and fighters. The contrast between battle and landing could not be more extreme: such was the bombers' war at that time.

The artist has used the road, trees and figures to enhance the perspective and to create a composition which is not only aesthetically very pleasing but also gives a good indication of scale. We can see how enormous the aircraft is, and how low it is flying on its final approach. Similarly, the towering mass of cumulus cloud serves to give a vertical scale, reaching as it does several miles high. Higher still is the operational ceiling of the aircraft where it has so recently battled with the enemy.

There is something particularly fascinating about aircraft coming in to land and this picture captures that moment of approaching the airfield boundary. The combination of creative imagery, golden English landscape and this most American of aircraft produces a truly memorable picture.

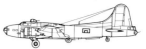

B-17G FORMATION *Gerald Coulson*
30 × 40in (76 × 101.5cm), oil.

This striking picture really does put you in the cockpit as this is exactly the view that would have been seen by the next aircraft down in the complex defensive boxes flown by B-17s. The theory behind these tight formations was to concentrate interlocking cones of fire from the many guns of each B-17 so that the formation could defend itself against fighter attacks (although in practice B-17s grew to depend on Mustang and Thunderbolt cover).

The B-17 has extremely beautiful lines and does not look dated. The wings have an aerodynamic cleanness with beautifully faired-in nacelles and neat wing-roots. Seen from this angle the right-hand wing has a stiletto-like appearance, further accentuating the aircraft's generally fine lines. The three gun-turrets, 'chin', ventral ball (underneath the fuselage), and mid-upper spoil the contours, but not so the tail turret, which is beautifully faired.

The B-17s are 'pulling con-trails' – streams of condensed water vapour from their exhausts which freeze at this high altitude (around 30,000ft). Flying and fighting this high seemed like scratching at the edge of space at the time. The natural aluminium finish of the aircraft stands out against the intense blue of the high-altitude sky. So too do the USAAF 'Stars and Bars' – a symbol as American as the Stars and Stripes.

This is certainly a fine painting of what a US pilot might term 'One mighty fine all-American airplane'.

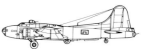

B-17 COASTAL COMMAND *Michael Turner*
12 × 16in (30.5 × 40.5cm), gouache.

Here we see the B-17 in a most unusual role – flying with Coastal Command of the RAF providing air cover for a convoy. At first glance this sort of 'double take' situation can be startling – a bit like seeing a Cadillac with a Union Jack on the door.

The sea has been caught particularly well and indeed looks just like the Atlantic with its huge ominous swells. This is very much a sailor's view of the aircraft which enhances our feeling of being part of the scene, on board a ship in this convoy. With the ever-present threat of U-boats the Allied sailors must have been immeasurably cheered by the sight of any friendly aircraft; a Guardian Angel against the deadly U-boat patrols.

WHEN THE EIGHTH MOVES IN *Gerald Coulson*
30 × 40in (76 × 101.5cm), oil.

This beautiful study of a B-17 is both nostalgic for those who remember when they operated from British bases and equally evocative for those who have seen examples at air shows – often from precisely this angle and in this wheels-and-flaps-down landing configuration.

Coulson has produced an exceptionally effective perspective by lowering the horizon and emphasising the stubble rows and indicating the relatively featureless characteristics of the field. The trees are on the horizon and seem very far away by virtue of their size relative to the figures in the middle-ground.

The beautiful shire-horses and the equally beautiful aircraft echo the 'ancient and modern' theme so beloved of aviation art. It also perhaps strikes a chord as evocative of Constable's 'Haywain', that quintessentially English painting. The ancient church on the horizon is yet another powerful symbol of the English rural idyll. The scene below is in stark contrast to this most American of aircraft sweeping through the sky.

The blip in history that for an instant brought together the ancient and the modern, the essence of America and Britain, is captured for ever in this stirring picture.

HEROES OF THE MIGHTY EIGHTH
Mark Postlethwaite
24 × 36in (61 × 91.5cm), acrylic on canvas.

The heroes of the title are both the airmen and the aircraft, such is the love enthusiasts and veterans alike have for these wonderful old aircraft. The aircraft illustrated are those flown by three famous Eighth Air Force pilots: Colonel Don Blakeslee (P51 Mustang), Colonel 'Hub' Zemke (P47 Thunderbolt) and Colonel William R. Lawley (B-17G Flying Fortress).

This picture is a very subtle blend of light and dark tones, coupled with the dramatic perspective of the condensation trails. Seen from this angle, the B-17 has a chunky, compact shape yet with slender and graceful lines. Note especially the tail-fin, the way the failing light just catches the propeller arcs, otherwise almost invisible, and how the central bosses of the propellers draw our eye to the dark discs of the radial aero engines. In close formation the gleaming Mustang, nearest to the mighty B-17, seems tiny. In company with it the heavy-bodied P-47 Thunderbolt seems dainty too, but this is the effect of perspective.

The cloudscape is interesting in that the central mass below the aircraft forms a triangular shape and the tones go from light to dark across the canvas from left to right. Thus the two fighters are silhouetted against a light background, whereas the B-17 is set-off against a dark background being lit from above.

The three aircraft are so positioned in formation that the angle between them and their contrails create a very strong perspective. Just as the Spitfire and the Lancaster were heroes of the RAF so here we have indeed three 'Heroes of the Mighty Eighth'.

'This painting was commissioned by my publishers "Skyscapes" to commemorate the fiftieth anniversary of US entry into World War II. My brief was simply to produce a symbolic painting depicting three famous aircraft: the B-17, P-51 and P-47.

I tried several sketches, mainly with two fighters in a vee formation with the bomber. However, these produced a confusing illusion of scale with one fighter always appearing larger than the bomber. I therefore arrived at this final composition, with the aircraft at high altitude and contrailing. To avoid the colour being too blue, I deliberately set the painting at a late sunset, thus enabling me to use a whole range of warm colours to contrast against the drab colouring of the bomber.'

MARK POSTLETHWAITE

MEMPHIS BELLE *Craig Kodera*
11 × 14in (28 × 35.5cm), oil on canvas.

The appeal of this type of painting lies at least partly in the fact that so many people have seen B-17s at air shows in just this 'low level pass' type of flight, although in this painting the aircraft is right 'on the deck'. The sound and sight of any four piston-engined aircraft is sadly becoming quite rare and it is now only at air shows that they can readily be experienced.

The composition of this most attractive painting is enhanced by the figures and the jeep in the foreground – again a classic triangular composition. The foreground details serve to add an element of nostalgia, giving the picture a more exact location in place and time – this is clearly a World War II Eighth Air Force base, in this case Bassingborne. As the figures and the jeep are relatively large we can see instantly how far away the B-17 is and how very much farther away is the formation waiting their turn to 'beat up' the field.

The bright lighting and clouds are typical of a good English summer's day and the light is used to good effect to bring out much fine detail on the aircraft. The painting is a record of 17 May 1943, when the Memphis Belle completed her twenty-fifth mission. The aircraft commander is Robert Morgan.

MORNING DEPARTURE *Gerald Coulson*
24 × 36in (61 × 91.5cm), oil.

The sight and sound of a fully-laden B-17 clawing its way into the morning air, all engines at full take off power, was and indeed still is an awesome event to behold. The artist has depicted a scene, so common during the war, when English skies regularly filled with swarms of American bombers and the air shook with the roar of their engines.

The aircraft depicted here stands out in sharp contrast to the bleak vastness of the airfield. In the far distance we can see numerous others taxiing into position to begin their take-off run in turn. Others are already in the air, wheeling and manoeuvring into their defensive box formations in readiness for their mission.

The artist has chosen to capture the tense moment of take off, when the aircraft is only just airborne. There is a wealth of fine detail in the aircraft, which is perfectly posed to show off its elegant lines.

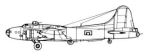

COMING HOME/ENGLAND 1943 *Gil Cohen*
22 × 44in (56 × 112cm), oil.

The atmosphere in this superb picture is electric. The faces of the men say it all: the aircrew know that they have put their lives 'on the line' and owe their safe return to the strength and resilience of each other and their B-17. The aircraft stands in silent witness to the battle they have just fought, peppered as it is with bullet holes from Luftwaffe fighters.

The picture is a composition built up of subgroups, each one of which tells a story. Two crew chiefs inspect the damage to the inboard engine nacelle of 'their' B-17, totally absorbed in the technicalities of the repair job. By way of contrast, next to them but oblivious of their presence, a lone crew member ducks under the fuselage

still visibly shocked and fatigued. The captain of the aircraft accepts a cigarette from the base commander. They touch hands in a ritual greeting, cigarettes and comradeship at that time being inextricably interwoven. The commander's adjutant looks on deep in thought, knowing how the crew feel at this moment. Two crewmen exchange silent glances and a comforting pat on the shoulder. Is it perhaps a gesture of thanks from one to the other for saving 'the ship' with a timely well-aimed burst from his guns just as a fighter was about to close in for the kill? A lone crewman gazes thoughtfully at the aircraft and beyond to a the formation circling overhead.

This evocative painting, displaying a wide range of reactions to the day's battle, is a fitting tribute to all combat airmen.

> 'This is a generic painting depicting a B-17 crew leaving their plane after a rough mission over Nazi-occupied Europe in late 1943. This was the dark time of the Schweinfurt/Regensburg missions, before the arrival of long-range fighters able to escort the bombers deep into enemy territory and return. Losses were very high and the entire concept of daylight precision bombing hung in the balance.'
>
> GIL COHEN

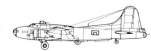

SCHWEINFURT BOUND *Jim Dietz*
32 × 48in (81.5 × 122cm), casein.

It is frequently said by veteran flyers that in the relatively brief duration of an aerial combat, when seconds seem like hours, the sky seems filled with aircraft. In this picture Jim Dietz has conveyed very well that feeling of a truly crowded sky. Such scenes as this, when hundreds of bombers stacked up in geometric formation patterns fought pitched battles with scores of enemy fighters, were unique to World War II. It is unlikely that such scenes will ever be seen again.

The artist has captured the absolute tumult of a running battle between B-17s and a mixture of Luftwaffe Me109s, twin-engined Me110s and Me410s. The rolling 109s are not engaging in displays of élan, but are rolling into the inverted position so that when they dive away they will be pulling positive 'g' – easier on the pilot and the airframe.

This picture challenges our imagination. We can readily imagine the excited shouts of the air gunners calling out their sightings of fighters – 'three o'clock, six o'clock . . . twelve o'clock high!' – and the staccato rattle of heavy-calibre machine guns. The Luftwaffe pilots would have been equally excited, and in their case boosted by the thought that they were flying over home territory.

Con-trails are everywhere, indicating that this is a high-altitude encounter in the freezing thin air of the stratosphere, where oxygen-masks and heated clothing are essential. The blue of the sky and the combination of wispy cloud and con-trail give the entire scene an air of other-worldliness so typical of high-altitude flight.

For any who may think that pictures such as this are artistic licence, exaggerations of reality, it is worth noting that there is much photographic and film evidence that stands silent witness to the authenticity and detailed accuracy of this fine painting.

B-17C *Richard Dann*
16 × 20in (40.5 × 51cm), oil on canvas.

The early models of the B-17 differed from those used by the Eighth Air Force in Europe in that they had a slender rear fuselage and small fin and rudder. Some would argue that it was these early models, as depicted here, which were aesthetically the more pleasing.

The B-17 in this picture is clearly a pre-war example bearing the red-and-white rudder-stripe, designed to resemble the American flag, and the wing-star with a red centre. The artist has posed the aircraft to show off to maximum advantage the beautiful slender fuselage and dainty fin and rudder.

The mountain in the background, Mount Rainier, Washington, became almost synonymous with Boeing aircraft which were frequently photographed flying over it. The intense blue sky and the con-trails coming from the B-17 in the background create an impression of very high-altitude flight. The turbo-charged engines of the B-17 conferred on it the ability to fly in the 'stratosphere' which became a buzzword of the time. By the standards of the day 'stratospheric flight' had the same ring to it as 'space flight' does now.

Richard Dann clearly has a great love for this particular B-17 model. By posing it as he has done, in its element at high altitude, he has revealed an aspect of this aircraft's history – its role in the development of flight – just as significant as its illustrious wartime record.

KELLY UNDER ATTACK *Jim Dietz*
20 × 30in (51 × 76cm), casein.

This dramatic picture depicts a scene at the very start of the B-17's career in World War II: the period covered by the movie *Airforce*, described elsewhere in this book. Strictly speaking, the actual debut of the B-17 was in July 1941 with RAF Bomber Command, flying against targets in France.

The B-17 in this painting – is partly cropped – thus enhancing the feeling of being very close in to the action. It is steeply banked, desperately manoeuvring in a sticky combat situation. The port outer has stopped, so we can see that the exchange of fire has begun to take effect. The remaining three engines are clearly straining at maximum power and the propeller discs are clear with only a yellow blur at the circumference. The attacking Mitsubishi zeros seem almost to be on an imminent collision course, unsettling enough for the bomber crew.

Although the picture is essentially a piece of representational art, with meticulous attention to detail (note, for example, the bullet holes in the fuselage and tail of the B-17), the background is quite impressionistic. The effective use of swirling colour creates a feeling of sky, land and cloud all mixed together, echoing the disorientation felt by the fighters.

Kelly Under Attack illustrates an action early in the American participation of the war, during which the B-17 pilot, Colin Kelly, won the first Congressional Medal of the War. After his aircraft had been severely damaged by attacking Zeros over Clark Field in the Philippines, he stayed at the controls long enough for his crew to bail out, sacrificing his life to do so. This painting was first published in a book entitled *Fortress in the Air.*

Schweinfurt Bound was originally done as a book cover on a book dealing with the history of the 305th Bomb Group stationed in England with the Eighth Air Force. It shows the B-17s of the Group being hit hard by the Luftwaffe on the Schweinfurt mission on 14 October 1943, before the advent of long range escort to and from the target; the 305th was the hardest hit group of that raid.

JIM DIETZ

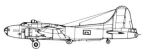

SAFE PASTURES *Mark Postlethwaite*
20 × 30in (51 × 76cm), acrylic on canvas.

The Swiss landscape is among the most beautiful in Europe and instantly recognisable. By putting the familiar in an unfamiliar setting the artist has created an eye-catching and very attractive picture.

Shot up and coming in for a belly-landing on only two engines, the B-17 swoops down on to an Alpine field. For the crew this means the end of their war, for in a neutral country belligerent airmen were usually interred for the duration. What mixed feelings would have gone through the minds of the crew as they considered their future?

Several B-17s in fact force-landed in Switzerland in similar circumstances to the one depicted here. Wheels-up forced landings were not a serious problem for the B-17 which, like many aircraft of the late 1930s, had in effect a semi-retractable undercarriage: the wheels protruding halfway out of the engine nacelles in the 'up' position to aid forced landings. However, fires were a possible hazard especially if fuel-tanks had been holed.

The artist has used the mountain and its snow covering to create a dramatic backdrop of light and dark directly behind the mostly silver-coloured aluminium aircraft. The mountains and hills create a pattern of triangles, jagged and rugged, contrasting starkly with the gracefully engineered lines of the bomber.

Belly-landings have a poignant drama all their own and evoke wartime memories of many a crippled aircraft struggling in 'on a wing and a prayer'. Not very frequently depicted in aviation art, this aspect of aerial warfare during World War II is faithfully portrayed here in a most unusual setting.

'The idea for this painting had been in my head for a very long time. A silver B-17, low amongst the beautiful scenery of Switzerland, was bound to make an attractive composition. Moreover, by showing the battle-ravaged bomber, struggling desperately for survival, against the tranquil background of a country still at peace, I wanted to convey the extreme and appalling contrasts that war can create.

Although over 150 aircraft came down in Switzerland during the war, it was impossible to research an actual B-17 that came down in a scene resembling this. Therefore a little artistic licence had to be used and I chose to illustrate an aircraft of the 92nd BG, a group that did lose several aircraft in the area at that time.'

MARK POSTLETHWAITE

B-17 *Geoffrey Lea*
20 × 30in (51 × 76cm), oil.

This tranquil depiction of a B-17 coming in to land at the end of its mission is the very antithesis of the scene depicted by Jim Dietz on page 54. The damage to the rudder, however, tells us that this aircraft has been in combat with enemy fighters. The World War II bombers which were based in Britain often experienced this extreme contrast of violent battle over enemy territory followed by a return to a rural England seemingly untouched by the war.

Tranquil as the scene is, our thoughts turn to the crew: are any wounded or even dead? how do they feel now the strain of risking their lives is lifted from their young shoulders (until the next mission)? The sound of the aircraft's tyres touching the runway must have been music to the ears of all bomber crews. We can readily imagine their forthcoming collective sigh of relief at that instant, now moments away, when the big war-bird lands on the English field.

The picture is a study of beautiful subtle muted soft tones, which is Geoffrey Lea's hallmark. The low-lying mist echoes the high wispy clouds where this aircraft has been at war and seems to blur the line between earth and air. The warming rays of the sun, glinting off its nose and the Plexiglas of the bombadier's position emphasise that this is indeed a machine built for flight.

This is a very romantic painting. It does not glorify war as such, but rather brings to us the wonderful beauty of an aircraft blending in perfectly with its setting.

B-17 FORMATION *Jim Laurier*
30 × 36in (76 × 91.5cm), oil on canvas.

The light in this picture has just the right quality for a scene set, as this is, relatively high with a view down on to tufts of cumulus clouds. The silver metal of the aircraft's skin has that beautiful shimmering quality that riveted-aluminium aircraft structures so characteristically possess.

It is noteworthy how much fine detail the artist has put into each aircraft at the same time posing them at just the right angle to show to best advantage the lovely symmetry of the B-17, always a most beautiful machine.

Jim Laurier's hallmark is his creative use of perspective to enhance the feeling of depth and three-dimensional space. It has been well brought out in this painting.

SALLY B *Michael Turner*
28 × 36in (71 × 91.5cm), acrylic.

This really lovely study is noteworthy for being a depiction of the *Sally B*, now famous as an air-show participant. Here we see *Sally* flying over a wartime Duxford complete with a con-trail criss-crossed sky.

American World War II aircraft were famous for their nose art – usually pin-up type nudes – and the *Sally B* is no exception save that in her case the nose art is relatively decorous.

The picture conveys very well the size of the B-17, one of the largest aircraft of its generation. The beautiful lines of the wing planform are set off to good advantage by

having the aircraft banked at this angle. The light just catching the yellow arcs of the propeller tips conveys perfectly the feeling of four huge piston aero engines roaring in deafening harmony. Modern aircraft may have more power, speed, weight and size, but few can match the B-17 for sheer impressive beauty. This fine painting certainly conveys that quality in full.

LONG AGO AND FAR AWAY *Jim Laurier*
18 × 24in (45.5 × 61cm), acrylic on board.

What a fascinating picture this is! By ingeniously putting together pictures within a picture plus artefacts – the shoulder-flashes and glasses – we immediately feel that we have stumbled across some treasure-trove of long-lost Glenn Miller memorabilia.

I personally find it quite impossible to look at pictures like this and not hear the band playing in my mind. The B-17, the Eighth Air Force, Glenn Miller and the USAAF Band are all closely interlinked. At many air shows Glenn Miller music is played when a B-17 makes an appearance.

The era preceding rock and roll will endure as the legend was set and sealed by fate when Glenn Miller flew to his untimely death just as the war was nearing its end. It is said that he had a premonition that he would never see America again and somehow there is a quality of wistfulness in his eyes as he looks at us across the years.

This is indeed a picture of 'Long Ago and Far Away', a nostalgic reminder for older hearts as they remember lost youth.

'"Long Ago and Far Away" is also the title of a popular song performed by Glenn Miller and the Army Air Force Band during many concerts overseas. General Eisenhower said Glenn Miller's band was the greatest morale booster for Allied troops next to a letter from home. "Ike" at least once, personally thanked Glenn and the boys for all they had done for the war effort. In this painting I tried to capture the mood of the time and the look of an airfield in England. Glenn Miller's music has transcended time, connecting the past with the present, as I have suggested with the glasses and shoulder-patches. Because of the continuing popularity of his music some of our finest memories of this era will last for many years to come.'

JIM LAURIER

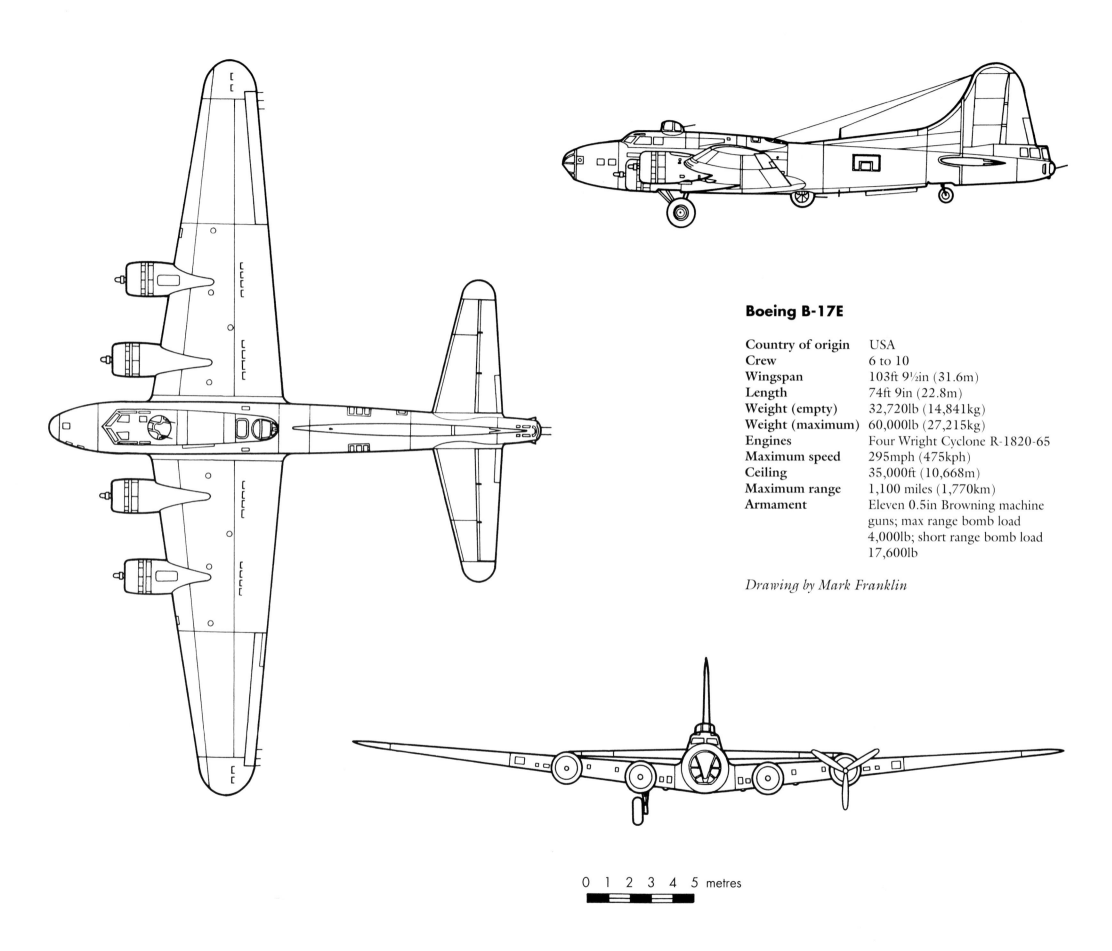

Boeing B-17E

Country of origin	USA
Crew	6 to 10
Wingspan	103ft 9½in (31.6m)
Length	74ft 9in (22.8m)
Weight (empty)	32,720lb (14,841kg)
Weight (maximum)	60,000lb (27,215kg)
Engines	Four Wright Cyclone R-1820-65
Maximum speed	295mph (475kph)
Ceiling	35,000ft (10,668m)
Maximum range	1,100 miles (1,770km)
Armament	Eleven 0.5in Browning machine guns; max range bomb load 4,000lb; short range bomb load 17,600lb

Drawing by Mark Franklin

0 1 2 3 4 5 metres

4 THE MESSERSCHMITT 109

Gerrman combat aircraft of the Second World War still evoke mixed emotions. German aeronautical art has yet to re-emerge, although there are many enthusiasts in that country. It is somewhat ironic that it often falls to British and American artists to depict German aircraft.

The reasons for this are perhaps to do with the all-pervasive nature of the Nazi state which cruelly misled and misused its people. Even today, art that evokes memories of that time can provoke powerful emotions and political argument among the German people.

The Messerschmitt 109 has a very Germanic, angular look. It seems to echo the steel helmet, Iron Cross and granite-jawed sculptures and posters, though this is merely a subjective impression. Early models *were* very angular, however, although later developments had more rounded contours to improve aerodynamics.

The aircraft was one of the all-time greats, capable of much modification and development. Developed in the 1930s, it flew on every battlefront throughout the war and the late models could still fly and fight with the best piston-engined fighters of 1945 – an achievement shared with the Spitfire, also of mid-1930s design. It was produced in larger numbers than any aircraft in history, approximately 33,000 in total – a staggering number. Its performance potential ensured it became the standard Luftwaffe fighter.

Just as with the Spitfire and other allied types, so too did the 109 have its aces: Mölders, Galland, Rall and others whose machines feature so much in the artwork. Most notable of the survivors is Adolf Galland, famous in his day for his cigar and Mickey Mouse with a hatchet emblem on the nose of his aircraft. His book *The First and the Last*, aptly titled, chronicles his experiences from the beginning to the end of the war, flying mainly in 109s.

One aspect of air combat in World War II, which made it a somewhat more 'noble' manifestation of war, was the intent to down the opponent's aircraft rather than to kill the aircrew. Obviously in the heat of battle

there was no time to 'aim to wound', but most combat pilots' memoirs stress that they flew with the wish to shoot down enemy *aircraft*. Time and again pilots write of seeing enemy aircraft burning out of control and automatically shouting to the crew to bail out. There were very few instances of airmen being shot at whilst parachuting to safety. War is horrific enough, but if conducted without chivalry it descends to the level of terrorism. Air combat between fighter pilots was the nearest thing in our age to the jousting of knights – and hence the legendary aces were often referred to as 'knights of the air'.

The paintings featured here justify the aviation en-

ADOLF GALLAND
Vic McLindon

thusiast's fascination with this superb fighter plane of World War II. In its many camouflage schemes it flew and fought on every battle front from the North African desert to the near-Arctic conditions of the Russian front. In both its early angular forms and its later more rounded versions this aircraft remained the leading aces' favourite throughout the war. The artists have caught this epic of aviation history in their dramatic and evocative paintings of this fine aeroplane.

GUNTHER RALL *Jim Laurier*
20 × 24in (51 × 61cm), prismacolor pencil on board.

Here the artist is painting not only from photo-reference but also from his own experience of meeting his subject. Unlike faces, eyes change relatively little through life and we see how well Laurier has caught their vitality and sparkle.

Also of note in this picture is the way the artist has captured the complexity of light and shadow in the cockpit produced by the open canopy frame and perspex panelling. The subject also actually *looks* as if he is sitting in a cockpit rather than just standing in front of a painted backdrop. Note the reflection in the lens of his goggles – a nice touch well executed.

'Gunther was among the most successful Messerschmitt pilots during World War II. In fact, he ended the war as the third highest-scoring ace of all time. He flew various models of the Bf109, primarily at the Eastern Front with JG52. I had the good fortune to meet Gunther at a fighter-ace and art symposium. He was a very youthful-looking and energetic man for his age, which made a lasting impression on me. This energy is clearly visible in his beaming smile and sparkling eyes. I'm sure it would have been just as interesting to know him as a young man as it was to meet him a few years ago.'

JIM LAURIER

ROMMEL'S ME109s *Peter Newton*
13½ × 20½in (34 × 52cm), watercolour and gouache.

This dramatic picture is doubly fascinating as it is painted directly from the artist's own experience. He observed this scene during his time with the 89th Regiment Royal Artillery in North Africa during World War II.

'The scene depicted in the painting took place approximately fifteen miles south of Tobruk. A tank battle had taken place some three hours previously. I had a heavy (0.5inch) machine gun, and although I was able to fire at the Messerschmitts I'm not sure if I hit one!

'The Messerschmitt 109 is such a beautiful aeroplane, and even at the time I greatly admired it. In a curious way I felt sorry when we hit one! I have tried to capture the dramatic moment when enemy aircraft suddenly flash overhead flying at very low altitude. It was a moment I shall never forget.'

PETER NEWTON

MESSERSCHMITT Bf109E-3 OF 1/JG3

Charles J. Thompson
10 × 14in (25.5 × 35.5cm), oil.

The early square-cut marks of the Me109 look especially rakish when viewed from this angle and they were frequently photographed from this direction. Thus by choosing this attitude Thompson is both showing the aircraft to best advantage and striking a chord with the aviation enthusiast.

The general angularity of the aircraft is not unattractive and is matched by the angularity of the German markings and the camouflage pattern. The yellow nose and rudder create a feeling of élan, the fighter pilot and fighter plane as knight and steed of the air.

The bright contrasting light emphasises the shape of the fuselage and wings, adding to the feeling of purposeful power and speed. This in turn is emphasised by the climbing/turning attitude of the aircraft.

This is the Messerschmitt of the early part of the war before its shape was rounded to improve it aerodynamically and all manner of gun-packs and other equipment were added. For many enthusiasts this is the 'classic' 109 of the Battle of Britain – arguably its finest hour.

ADOLF GALLAND *Michael Turner*
16 × 20in (40.5 × 51cm), gouache.

Flying is synonymous with speed but ironically the greatest sense of speed occurs when aircraft are flying at their slowest: at take-off and landing. The leading aircraft is that of Adolf Galland, arguably the most famous of all the German World War II aces, and we can clearly see his emblem on the side of the fuselage: Mickey Mouse brandishing an axe.

A subtle feature is the way all three aircraft are shown very slightly rocking. Fighter aircraft of this period, and especially the 109s, were something of a handful on take-off and required skill and concentration to fly. This feeling of the machines swaying in the air as they rush across the field gathering speed is well caught.

ADOLF GALLAND'S MESSERSCHMITT 109
Mark Postlethwaite
30 × 24in (76 × 61cm), acrylic on canvas.

This fine study of a '109' beautifully reveals the rakish lines of this classic fighter. The artist has posed the aircraft to perfection; he has chosen one of the best views possible. The dramatic and dynamic effects in this picture have been enhanced by lowering the horizon to less than a third from the bottom edge.

The yellow spinner and rudder is picked up in the clouds and the land. The clouds are arranged in a formation that frames the aircraft, in a manner reminiscent of a halo.

The artist has caught the propeller blur with delicate subtlety in a way that conveys the feeling of a climbing turn with full power. Adolf Galland and his aircraft are much-painted subjects, as he is a legendary figure: in some ways he is considered to be the Richthofen of World War II. Mark Postlethwaite has successfully created a fresh and stimulating picture on a popular theme.

ONE TO ONE *Ivan Berryman*
14 × 20in (35.5 × 51cm), acrylic on canvas.

This study of a Messerschmitt Bf109E of JG27 closing on a 501 Squadron Hawker Hurricane during a typical combat over southern England in the summer of 1940 is a fascinating and most unusual picture. The artist has presented us with a very spectacular view of a 109. Any model-aircraft enthusiast will at some stage have had the pleasure of viewing his or her creation from unusual angles such as this, either as part of the building process or just out of curiosity. Here we have that sort of modeller's-eye view of the 109. Pictures like this give us a better sense of knowing the aircraft inside-out and from all angles. They also add something new and fresh to a subject we thought we already knew all about. Such ingenious approaches to familiar subjects prevent them from becoming stale or hackneyed.

The almost technical illustration style is very pleasant and easy on the eye. The nuts, bolts and fine details make this essentially a study of the machine with the pilot in the cockpit very much in the background.

'As a professional photographer who frequently took air-to-air photographs of aircraft, I was often frustrated by the practical impossibility of getting in as close as I would like in order to gain dizzying viewpoints with spectacular perspectives. As an artist, I can do anything I like in a free and unlimited way. Although the sky is a vast open space and often lonely too, in this painting I have tried to capture the crowded effect of an air combat.'

IVAN BERRYMAN

Ivan Berryman '89

'This venture into the abstract freed me from the confines of figurative accuracy normally associated with aircraft painting. An outstanding machine of historical significance the Bf109E, known as the Emil, has distinctive tailplane struts and a unique profile which, together with an impressive charisma and menacing appearance of ruthless efficiency, combines to make a fertile subject for abstract adventure.

By using a front elevation any reference to the political swastika is excluded. Showing two aircraft gives a valuable opportunity to develop depth through size, as well as by colour and tone, in the otherwise two-dimensional layout. Lines radiating from the spinner centres create an exploding pattern, while angular shapes and straight lines contrast with the overlapping circles of the propellers, adding to the impression of power, speed and sound which express the dynamic essence of the Bf109E. A limited palette gives unity to the composition yet permits symbolic suggestions of sky and earth dominated by the aircraft.

The acceptance of the painting as aviation art or as a piece of pure decoration is left to the observer.'

PETER G. NIELD

EMIL – EMIL *Peter Nield*
18 × 22in (45.5 × 56cm), oil.

Deriving his style from Cubism, Peter Nield has nevertheless produced an extremely recognisable and accurate portrayal of the Me109. All the angularity and menace of the aircraft is there with, on close examination, a fair amount of accurate technical detail such as gun-ports, air-intakes and so forth. The whole is a study of straight lines with two circles (the propeller arcs, one of which is cut by the picture frame). Sky is indicated by sectors of blue and grey, land by browns and greens.

The style is well suited to the subject as it is more than slightly reminiscent of the Bauhaus movement in Germany, which influenced aircraft companies and airlines at least in terms of buildings and interior design. This picture challenges our conception of both the boundaries of aviation art, and how far we will go in search of art that 'speaks' to us of the subject we love. For those reasons alone it deserves inclusion in this book.

WERNER MÖLDERS *Michael Turner*
16 × 24in (40.5 × 61cm), gouache.

This dramatic picture shows Luftwaffe ace Werner Mölders shooting down a Curtis Hawk of L'Armée de l'Air in France. It is unusual in that few artists depict aircraft in the process of actually crashing.

Because the action is taking place at very low altitude, the speed effect is very marked – as it is in scenes depicting take-offs. The angle at which the Messerschmitt is banked shows off its beautiful if angular lines and the symmetry of the wing planform. This view is one familiar to enthusiasts who attend air displays.

Swooping low in turning flight to show off an aircraft to best effect is a classic manoeuvre. Here it also echoes a feeling of elation in victory. While all this is happening, the soldiers in the tank have a grandstand view of the aerial battle raging overhead, several of whose participants continue to wheel and turn in the background.

THE STRAGGLER *Frank Wootton*
25 × 36in (63.5 × 91.5cm), oil.

Speed and drama characterise Frank Wootton's exciting picture. The Me109 is in a truly classic pose for a fighter plane banked up steeply as it turns in an attempt to get on to the tail of the pursuing Spitfire while below a damaged B-17, one engine out, runs for home.

The painting has a pleasing classic triangular composition, which also helps to create and enhance perspective. The B-17 appears to be both distant and beneath us. The slight hint of an exhaust-smoke trail from the Me109 is very effective. As with a 'speed streak' or a wing-tip vortex it enhances the impression of high-speed flight.

Perhaps the most notable and interesting feature of this painting is its style. The feel of speed, use of colour and composition mark it out instantly as a Frank Wootton. This artist has been painting aircraft in a distinctive manner for over fifty years. During World War II he had the opportunity to see the aircraft he loves at first hand, when he was an official war artist.

THE HIGH TIDE OF SUMMER *Jim Laurier*
24 × 36in (61 × 91.5cm), acrylic on board.

This is a slightly unusual picture in that we are looking at
the aircraft from the tail. It is highly effective, however, in
that the angle of the fuselage and wings draws our eye to
the focus of the picture, namely the group of figures. Also,
because the aircraft is a tailwheel type, the fuselage is
inclined upwards and points arrow-like to the sky – its

natural element. This heroic quality is enhanced by the
figures themselves being silhouetted against the sky.

Their enthusiasm is evident not just by their smiles but
also by their eager springing movements and alert
postures. We feel drawn to the group by a kind of
magnetism which all aviation enthusiasts feel in this
situation. Oh to have been there – in the picture! The pilot
in this painting is Gunther Rall, surrounded by his
'schwarzmen', or ground crew.

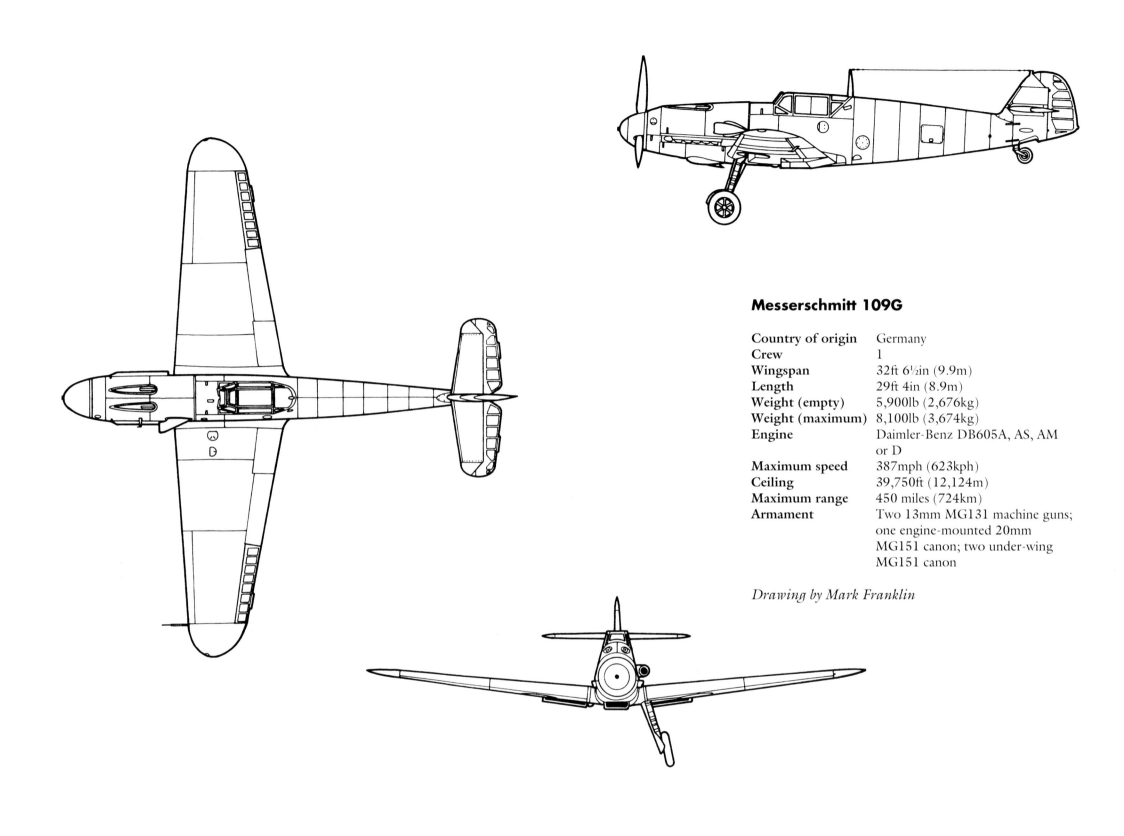

Messerschmitt 109G

Country of origin	Germany
Crew	1
Wingspan	32ft 6½in (9.9m)
Length	29ft 4in (8.9m)
Weight (empty)	5,900lb (2,676kg)
Weight (maximum)	8,100lb (3,674kg)
Engine	Daimler-Benz DB605A, AS, AM or D
Maximum speed	387mph (623kph)
Ceiling	39,750ft (12,124m)
Maximum range	450 miles (724km)
Armament	Two 13mm MG131 machine guns; one engine-mounted 20mm MG151 canon; two under-wing MG151 canon

Drawing by Mark Franklin

5 THE P-51 MUSTANG

The name 'Mustang' is perfect for this aircraft. The image it conjures up of a galloping horse, mane flowing in the wind, tail streaming out behind, is exactly right: the aircraft is the very embodiment of grace and speed. And like its equine namesake, the aerial Mustang of World War II is a creature we can relate to and understand.

No finer illustration of this is to be found than in a sequence from Steven Spielberg's *Empire of the Sun* (see page 16). In a truly magic moment of cinematography the young hero leaps up and down with unbridled enthusiasm as the Japanese airfield next to his prison camp is strafed by P-51s. 'Cadillac of the skies, Cadillac of the skies!' he shouts repeatedly (echoing a description he has read in a magazine). The Mustangs blaze away with their six 'fifties', decimating the few outclassed Zeros that attempt to attack them. Myth, movie and pop-art comic strip combine and the boy hero is a metaphor for all aviation enthusiasts.

Mustangs still survive and every year at the truly wondrous air races held at Reno, Nevada, they can be seen roaring around the aerial racetrack at near-zero altitude. How apt that they should live on in yet one more dimension of the equestrian analogy – Mustang: the racehorse of the skies! Just as galloping hooves quicken the pulse so these aerial racers' Merlins roar with a sound that oozes power and vibrant energy. Sunlight glints on their highly polished metal wings and canopies, for they are all groomed as thoroughbreds for both beauty and maximum speed. If any man–machine event can bring a lump to the throat then surely it must be this one!

The Mustang is one of the truly great aircraft of all time and a triumph of modification over mediocrity. Originally conceived of by the RAF who drew up the specification and powered by an Allison engine intended for low-level support/army co-operation duties, it was a compact, clean design but with mediocre performance. What transformed it was the installation of a Rolls-Royce Merlin engine.

The Merlin engine revolutionised the Mustang as it was designed to perform at altitude whereas the Allison was optimised for low-altitude performance, it being anticipated by the USAAF that the Mustang would be used more for ground support than high-altitude combat. It is worth recording that the Merlin, at the time it was first fitted to the Mustang, had itself been radically improved by a brilliant young engineer at Rolls-Royce, Stanley Hooker. An expert in fluid mechanics, he set about redesigning the supercharger fitted to the Merlin (the engine-driven paddle compressor which fed the engine compressed air) thereby boosting its power, especially at altitude. Hooker's vital work won him a richly deserved knighthood.

The first Merlin-powered Mustangs (September 1942) were nearly twice as fast to 20,000ft – 5.9 minutes compared with 9.1 minutes. Top speed was a stunning 441mph, some 60mph faster than with the Allison engine. Most significant of all, with extended internal fuel tanks the Mustang had a tremendous range and with drop tanks added could escort American daylight bombers over all of occupied Europe.

Mustangs escorted B-17s and B-24s on missions deep into German-held territory. They systematically decimated the day-fighter force of the Luftwaffe throughout 1944. In the closing stages of the war German day-fighter defences were virtually non-existent. Mustangs also fought on most fronts, including the Pacific, escorting bombers and fighting in a ground-attack/close-support role. The RAF also operated Mustangs in large numbers and for a wide variety of roles. Mustangs fought on in Korea and served with many air forces throughout the 1950s. Of all World War II fighters, it survives in the largest numbers and is the mainstay of much air racing and numerous private collections and museums.

Fast, manoeuvrable, strong, well armed and with a tremendous range, the P-51 Mustang was a superb achievement in its day. Its angular look suggests a family connection with the Messerschmitt 109; however, con-

ROBIN OLDS *David Hamm*

Born in Honolulu on 14 July 1922, Robin Olds (the son of Robert C. Olds – a USAAC pilot who became a Brigadier General) graduated from West Point in 1940. In May 1944 he was posted overseas with 479 Fighter Group, the last fighter group to be assigned to the Eighth Air Force in Europe.

Originally equipped with P38 Lightnings – with which Olds scored nine victories – the group was re-equipped with P-51D Mustangs in September 1944. In January 1945 he took command of 479 Fighter Group's 434 Fighter Squadron. By VE Day he had completed 107 combat missions and had a score of 24½ victories,* thus becoming the 479's top-scoring ace.

His post-war career included tours in England, Korea and Vietnam where he scored four more victories in air combat. Olds finished his career as a Commandant of Cadets at the Air Force Academy at Colorado Springs, retiring with the rank of Brigadier General.

---

* Half a victory is recorded when two aircraft engage a single aircraft and it is not clear which pilot is responsible for the victory. This can also occur when an anti-aircraft battery fires at an aircraft being attacked by another aircraft at the same time.

trary to popular myth, Edgar Schimued the Chief Designer at North American Aviation had never worked for Messerschmitt. This simplicity of line aided mass production. Not only is the entire aircraft a very neat, simple shape, it is also very 'clean'. The radiator under the fuselage leaves the nose uncluttered. Most Mustangs had 'bubble' hoods and cut-down rear fuselages, which markedly improved the pilot's rear view. It also further enhanced the generally precise, pleasing lines of the aircraft.

The design has stood the test of time exceptionally well; even in the 1990s it looks modern. Turbo-prop training aircraft seem to be making a comeback, and many of these have neat, angular lines similar to the Mustang. There is none of the 1930s teardrop streamlining which now seems so dated. This was in fact a crude approach to design, ignoring as it does the 'wetted area' (the surface area of an aircraft subjected to the flow of air in flight; while teardrop streamlining reduces drag, it can also *increase* drag by increasing the wetted area). This is kept to a minimum in the Mustang, while areas requiring streamlining, for example nose contours, are kept very smooth. The 'fit' of wings and tail is very satisfying both aesthetically and aerodynamically. There are no 'lashed-up' fairings around the wing roots – everything is correct in both appearance and function. The net result is a superb, strong, fast aeroplane that handles wonderfully and was easy to manufacture.

Numerous aces have written of their love for this little plane. Chuck Yaeger, the man famous for being the first to break the sound barrier in 1947 and one of the world's foremost test pilots, wrote very highly of it in his biography *Yaeger*. Flying Mustangs he became a top-scoring USAAF pilot during the war. As a test pilot he had the opportunity to fly nearly every German fighter in the USA just after the war, yet he rated only the Focke-Wulf 190 as being the equal of the American Mustang.

It is only natural, therefore, that this aircraft has become such a popular subject for artists. It is a living example of the breed, a true World War II fighter plane still seen at many air shows, thus readily accessible in both flying and static states. Added to this is the fact that many of them were painted in very distinctive colour schemes, often with names and pin-up girls painted on their engine cowlings. All these factors combine to make this aircraft a most attractive subject for aviation artists both past and present.

GEORGE PREDDY *Jim Laurier*
20 × 24in (51 × 61cm), Prismacolor pencil on board.

The fighter pilot has, since the dawn of air warfare, caught the public imagination. As advancing technology made chivalry on the ground less possible, so it restored it in the air.

This fine study captures well the enthusiasm and vitality of all fighter pilots. Generally speaking, they all possess the same qualities as racing drivers – skill, nerve, high levels of concentration and also team spirit. In a world very short on heroes, many fighter pilots certainly measure up.

This picture is also of great technical nostalgic interest in that the flying clothing is World War II American Army Air Force issue. Needless to say, all such clothing and equipment, redolent as it is of this whole era, is now sought after by collectors. As with all good portraits, the personality shines through very strongly and stays in the memory.

'I chose George Preddy as my subject because his was one of the most interesting stories of World War II. It reads like a screenplay from a Hollywood movie. As a young man he was frail in appearance, but determined to fly and be a fighter pilot. He struggled to overcome many adversities and not only succeeded in becoming an aviator, but quickly soared to the top of the list of Mustang aces. He was the best, although very modest about it. He was celebrated as a hero in the United States and then, tragically, he was accidentally shot down and killed by US anti-aircraft fire on Christmas Day 1944. Had he not requested several extensions of combat duty, he would have survived the war. It makes one wonder what heights he might have risen to during the remainder of his life and what part, if any, fate plays in our lives.'

JIM LAURIER

GONE HUNTIN' *Craig Kodera*
18 × 24in (45.5 × 61cm), oil on canvas.

High speed at low level, a small fighter at its most
dramatic! The effect of dramatic speed is enhanced by the
banked angle of the aircraft and the inclination of the
horizon in the opposite direction. Together, they create a

strong feeling of high-speed turns with the consequent
'G'-loading on aircraft and pilot.

On the ground below Luftwaffe Me110's, caught
unawares, are the victims of this marauding P-51. This
ground-attack aspect of the fighter pilot's role is not very
often the subject of aviation art. Less obviously heroic than
air-to-air combat, it was a vital aspect of the air war and

not without its risks from ground-fire. The 355th Fighter
Group pioneered the ground attack role. This aircraft is
flown by Captain Henry W. Brown, the leading US ace in
Europe in 1944.

RENO RACER *Charles J. Thompson*
36 × 24in (91.5 × 61cm), oil.

This stunning picture of a P-51 Mustang depicted in this distinctive way, which is very much the hallmark of Charles Thompson, makes a fascinating comparison with his similar painting of a P-47 Thunderbolt (see page 89).

Once again the Mustang seems a completely new shape, and being a post-war Reno racer it is now in bright-red racing trim with coloured stripes and decorations. Purists will be quick to notice, however, that the cockpit has been modified to cut down drag and is no longer the familiar bubble hood of the P-51D.

Polished and tuned to perfection, stripped of all armour, guns and ammunition, aircraft like this can attain the ultimate in piston-engined performance. In 1983 this particular machine, flown by Frank Taylor, set a world record over a set course at Mojave of 517.06mph.

Mustangs live on as racers in America, still capable of outstanding performance scarcely equalled by any similar racing aircraft of modern design. This is an amazing aspect of the aircraft and the farsightedness of its designers fifty years ago. In his picture the artist has captured the sleek angularity of this wonderful old aircraft in his own inimitable manner.

NORMANDY *Michael Turner*
12 × 16in (30.5 × 40.5cm), gouache.

Sometimes a composition in aviation art is such that the aircraft can be almost secondary to another theme. Here is an example of such a painting; in it the anti-aircraft gun is more prominent than the aircraft.

There is, however, a link between the two elements in the picture. Both the gun and its crew's gaze are trained skywards, anxiously anticipating an attack. The Mustang is leaving urgently to photograph enemy positions. There is certainly a dramatic question implicit in this picture and the viewer is drawn into the action.

The Mustang is a little unusual in that it is in RAF markings and is an early model dating from before the Mustang was fitted with a Rolls Royce Merlin engine. It also appears to have unusually long undercarriage legs. This is because the aircraft is just lifting off the ground and the oleo legs are fully extended as they no longer support its weight. At the angle the artist has painted it the aircraft's delicate, almost fragile contours are shown off to great effect. The dust being thrown up by its prop-wash adds to the feeling of speed and movement.

P-51 MUSTANGS *Michael Turner*
16 × 24in (40.5 × 61cm), gouache.

Traffic jams on the road are familiar enough – but on an aerodrome! This was, however, a common enough sight on Allied air bases in World War II. Strictly speaking of course not a jam as such, just aircraft in their dozens jockeying for position in what would be a take-off in formations of three or four.

One of the attractions of a picture such as this is the impression of power that it conveys to anyone who has stood and watched such a sight as this. Apart from the sheer spectacle of the event, it is the *sound* of all the piston aero engines which is so wonderful. Today the nearest we can come to experiencing this is at an air show or the air races held annually at Reno, Nevada.

The artist has a very free, bold style but also incorporates much fine detail. The cockpit detail in the bubble-hood Mustang is particularly noteworthy.

DESTINATION GERMANY *Ronald Wong*
18 × 27in (45.5 × 69cm), acrylic.

This fine study of two Mustangs taking off is very atmospheric, combining as it does both aircraft and GIs in the ubiquitous jeep, trademark of the American armed forces. The group of figures at the jeep provides a counterpoint to the two aircraft. The figures are seemingly fixed and unmoving, attached to terra firma. They are the very opposite of the two aircraft which are racing at ever-increasing speed into their element, the intangible air. There is a certain magic about flying which is always fascinating, however much an individual may fly or see

aircraft. No amount of technical knowledge can ever completely explain away the wonder and miracle of flight.

The group at the jeep also help to anchor this instant in history – this is not an airshow but the finest hour of the Mustang, when for a brief moment in time it flew high above Germany defending the American daylight bombers. The picture gives us a refreshing new impression of the Mustang which emphasises its delicacy of line and its shimmering silver body. Clearly it is of that element – the sky – whereas the jeep and the figures are of the grass and dark earth.

The use of red in both the sky and the earth complement each other well, suggesting again the two

elements of earth and air, reflecting and harmonising with each other. The feeling of space is well portrayed in this picture; the detail of the hangar is very small, emphasising the seemingly huge flatness of the airfield. The jeep in the foreground appears to be the same size as the nearest aircraft, thus placing the relatively large aircraft in perspective at a distance. This effect is enhanced by the jeep and aircraft wings aligning to the same vanishing point.

This is a lovely atmospheric picture which portrays the Mustang in a refreshingly new way by use of subtlety of composition and, above all, colour.

LOOKING FOR TROUBLE *Robert Watts*
24 × 36in (61 × 91.5cm), oil on linen.

This classic 'stacked up' formation often featured in aircraft photographs in the 1930s and 1940s. Later, improved fighter tactics replaced it but it is always a dramatic and eye-catching arrangement for a painting of a group of aircraft.

Robert Watts has created some lovely soft subtle tones in this painting, which are reminiscent of British artists although in fact he is American. The choice of landscape is very effective – the S-shaped river really does appear to be winding away into the distance, and he has created a good feeling of depth by the careful use of tone and colour.

The composition has a heightened degree of realism in that the aircraft are not posed artificially but are slightly

bunched together, the outline of one just overlapping the outline of the next. This also has the effect of softening the very angular shape of the Mustang, an attractive and modern-looking quality of this aircraft. It is also interesting to note how the aircraft formation and the winding river create a triangular composition. As with the landscape, the aircraft also fade with distance in a very subtle and pleasing way.

MUSTANG MK I *Frank Wootton*
22 × 30in (56 × 76cm), oil.

Speed is the theme of this exciting study of a Mustang in
RAF markings, swooping down at high velocity. To
emphasise the feeling of speed Wootton has blurred not
only the background but also the aircraft itself, though
only very slightly. This is an old technique for depicting
speed which was often used to good effect when
portraying fast-moving aircraft and vehicles. Not so
common today, this technique is still used by the artist
who perfected it many years ago.

To emphasise the feeling of speed even more the
propeller blade shimmer is bent back, as if forced into this
position by the slipstream. This is the machine-age
equivalent of the horse's mane flowing in the wind.

In the background the rows of trees, fields and so forth
are aligned to the aircraft's direction of flight. The road
runs parallel with the leading edge of the Mustang's wings
and various buildings and other details are aligned parallel
to the tailplane. There is great symmetry in this picture
which creates a feeling of harmony and balance. It is also
notable how light and dark areas balance and also serve to
emphasise the colour and shape of the aircraft. To add
drama to the scene a tracer snakes up from the ground and
flak explodes uncomfortably close.

This is a very atmospheric picture which is characterised
by the artist's own very strong style. He paints not only
with a profound skill developed through long experience,
but also with tremendous depth of feeling.

BLAKESLEE BEFORE BERLIN *Jim Dietz*
30 × 40in (76 × 101.5cm), oil.

This highly atmospheric painting captures the tension of
those last moments before the start of a mission. It depicts
the 4th US Fighter Group at Debden before the first
American raid on Berlin, 4 March 1944. The pilot of the
P-51 featured is Colonel Donald J. M. Blakeslee.

Enthusiasts will note that Blakeslee's Mustang is a little
unusual in that it is one of the few fitted with the
'Malcolm' hood similar to that on most Spitfires. All the
other aircraft are early models with hinging canopies.

The Fourth Fighter Group, nicknamed the
Blakesleewaffe, was one of the most successful American
Fighter Groups serving with the Eighth Air Force in
England, and claimed over 1,000 German aircraft
destroyed during its service there.

P-51 MUSTANG *Geoffrey Lea*
20 × 30in (51 × 76cm), oil.

There is a timeless beauty to the Mustang which is forever
new and fresh. This effect is of course enhanced by the
continued production of aircraft in the training and exec-
utive categories which bear a marked resemblance to it.

The cloudscape in this lovely picture sets off the
Mustang well. The backdrop of cumulus cloud with
dramatic sunrays bursting through literally serves to
spotlight the aircraft, setting off glinting highlights on the
perspex canopy and natural metal skin. Far below is a
cloud-bank looking very like the waves of the sea, a most
beautiful effect frequently seen from the air. Between these
two backdrops flies the red-nosed Mustang, banking
gently towards us. The perspective effect of the clouds
below and the sun's rays combine to almost project the
aircraft out from the canvas.

What at first glance might seem to be an aircraft portrait,
on closer examination is, in fact, a most dramatic painting
full of dynamic movement and glowing colour.

P-51B MUSTANG, 371 FIGHTER SQUADRON
Ernest Nisbet
14 × 17in (35.5 × 43cm), gouache.

This artist has a very striking style and specialises in using gouache. In this picture he has chosen to depict an early model P-51B Mustang escorting a Martin B-26B Marauder. The picture is characterised by a delicacy and lightness to which the medium lends itself. The typical high-altitude cirrus clouds enhance the feeling of speed and movement, which is further emphasised by the angle between the two aircraft.

The natural aluminium finish of the aircraft serves to reflect ambient light and colour, thereby enhancing the feeling that the aircraft are part of their natural element – the sky.

This is a most attractive painting in a style very characteristic of this artist and as such makes for an interesting comparison with other P-51 paintings.

THE HUN HUNTER OF TEXAS, CAPTAIN HENRY BROWN *Craig Kodera*
15 × 30in (38 × 76cm), oil on canvas.

The speed and power of the superb Mustang are captured marvellously in this study. One can almost hear the roar of the engine as this little fighter streaks along 'on the deck' at top speed. This impression of speed is enhanced by the steeply inclined horizon which gives a feeling of the aircraft going 'downhill', even though it is clearly just starting to climb.

The aircraft is posed such that we are viewing it almost in silhouette, a view that shows off well the sleek contours of the Mustang's fuselage. The detail is very fine and we can clearly see the pilot under the bubble-hood looking towards us. The propeller is almost invisible as it spins at high revs with just the hint of a streak at its edge.

Both this study and Kodera's 'Hun Hunter' on page 75 are very fine examples of photo-realism in aviation art, which are also characterised by their bright, sharp contrast and fine detail. They are very much the stuff of dramatic, high-speed flying at low altitude, with a superb little fighter plane as their subject. As such they make for an interesting comparison with some of the other pictures in this book.

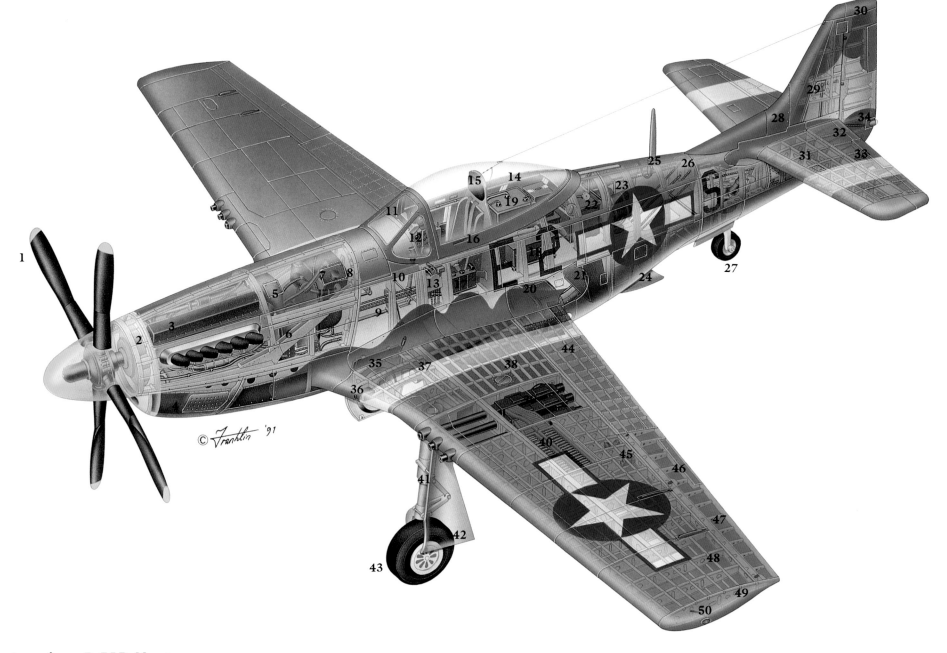

North American P-51D Mustang

1	Hamilton standard hydromatic propeller
2	Cooling liquid tank
3	Packard-built V-1650-7 Rolls-Royce Merlin liquid cooled V12 engine
4	Carburettor air duct
5	Intercooler for two-stage supercharger
6	Engine mounting
7	Oil tank
8	Front armoured bulkhead
9	Rudder pedals
10	Control column
11	Bell & Howell N9 gunsight
12	Electrical circuit indicator panel
13	Throttle quadrant
14	Cockpit canopy
15	Headrest and rear armoured bulkhead
16	Canopy external opening lever
17	Trim, rudder, aileron and carburettor controls
18	Radio compartment
19	Battery
20	Oil radiator
21	Coolant radiator
22	Fuselage auxiliary fuel tank, 322 litres
23	Oxygen bottles
24	Adjustable air outlet
25	Aerial mast
26	Rear bulkhead and fuselage joint
27	Retractable tail wheel
28	Tailfin
29	Rudder tab cable
30	Rudder
31	Stabiliser
32	Elevator
33	Elevator trim tab actuator
34	Navigation light
35	Undercarriage doors
36	Gun camera
37	Landing light
38	Main wing fuel tank, 348 litres
39	Colt Browning .50 calibre machine guns
40	Ammunition boxes, 400 rounds inner gun, 270 rounds outer guns
41	Undercarriage shock absorber
42	Undercarriage door
43	Undercarriage wheel
44	Alclad covered flaps
45	Trim tab servo
46	Trim tab
47	Aileron
48	Wing structure
49	Detachable wing-tip
50	Navigation light

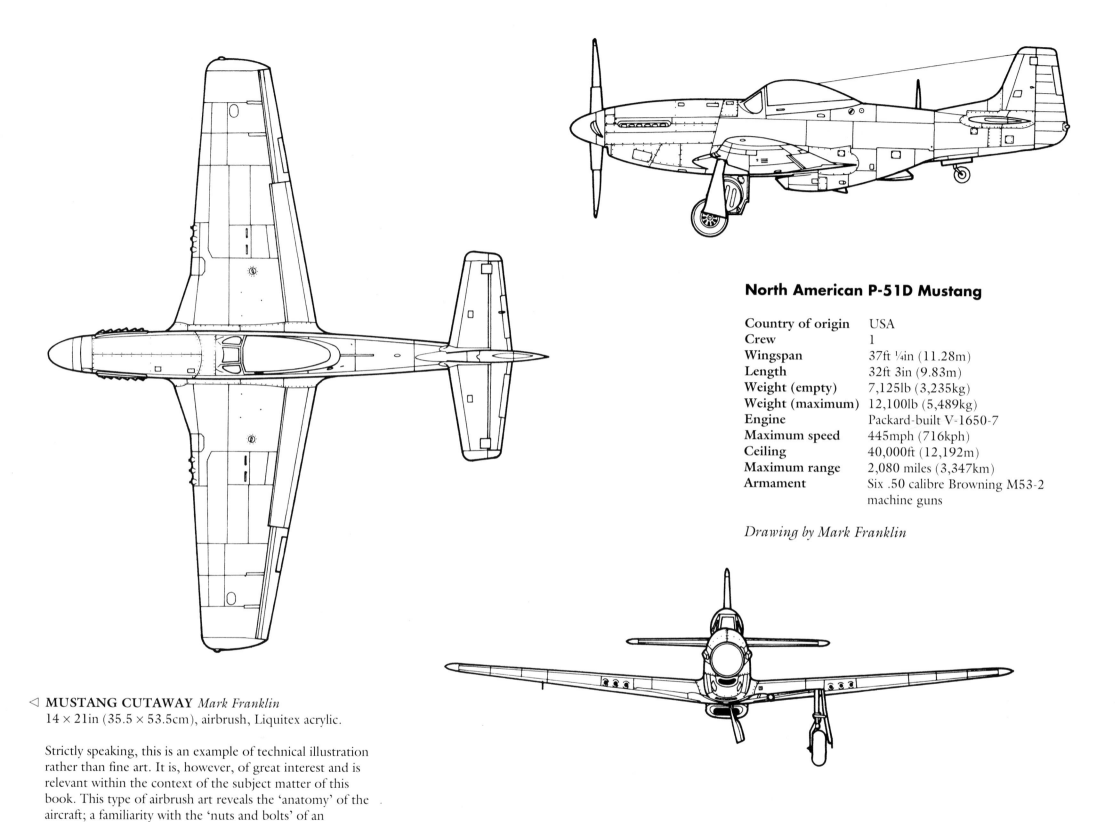

North American P-51D Mustang

Country of origin	USA
Crew	1
Wingspan	37ft ¼in (11.28m)
Length	32ft 3in (9.83m)
Weight (empty)	7,125lb (3,235kg)
Weight (maximum)	12,100lb (5,489kg)
Engine	Packard-built V-1650-7
Maximum speed	445mph (716kph)
Ceiling	40,000ft (12,192m)
Maximum range	2,080 miles (3,347km)
Armament	Six .50 calibre Browning M53-2 machine guns

Drawing by Mark Franklin

◁ **MUSTANG CUTAWAY** *Mark Franklin*
14 × 21in (35.5 × 53.5cm), airbrush, Liquitex acrylic.

Strictly speaking, this is an example of technical illustration rather than fine art. It is, however, of great interest and is relevant within the context of the subject matter of this book. This type of airbrush art reveals the 'anatomy' of the aircraft; a familiarity with the 'nuts and bolts' of an aeroplane is important for both artist and art lover. This cutaway clearly shows how the Mustang is constructed and what it is like beneath its skin. The form of the surface hints at the structures which lie beneath, in the same way that the muscles and skeleton can be seen beneath the skin of a human figure or animal.

0   1   2   3   4   5   metres

6 THE REPUBLIC P-47 THUNDERBOLT

If reincarnation exists for machines then the Thunderbolt was probably a V-12 Cadillac in its previous life! It was very big, powerful, heavy, fast and packed a terrific punch. An awesome weapon in its time, it is still impressive half a century on.

If aircraft like the Spitfire and Mustang call to mind the sleek, athletic beauty of the racehorse, what then the Thunderbolt? Sleek and graceful it was not, but it was no carthorse either. Its wing had the elliptical planform like that of the Spitfire. Similarly, the fin and rudder, tailplane and elevators had a graceful pre-war-styled curvature. It is of course the fuselage and engine which so dominate the overall appearance of the aircraft.

The P-47D was powered by a Pratt and Whitney R-2800-59 Double Wasp 18 cylinder two-row radial engine of 2,000hp (2,300hp at 31,000ft). This was heavyweight power – by comparison, the Rolls-Royce Merlin (as fitted to Spitfires and Mustangs) weighed 1,500lb whereas the Double Wasp weighed 2,280lb; the former had a capacity of 27 litres whereas the latter's was 45 litres! To absorb this massive amount of power a 12ft diameter airscrew with four blades was fitted. This in turn required the undercarriage legs to extend 9in when lowered, in order to provide sufficient ground clearance. Larger undercarriage legs would have interfered with the wing space allocated for the armament.

Buried in the rear fuselage was the large exhaust-driven supercharger and intercooler, exhausting via gates on the fuselage sides. This complex ducting of hot gases under pressure, turbine technology and control added up to over half a jet engine. All that was lacking was a combustion chamber instead of a piston engine. As Glyn Jones put it:

One trick . . . they [the General Electric turbo-supercharger development engineers led by Sandford Moss] missed. Their turbo-superchargers compressed engine gases and cold air between centrifugal compressors and turbine and then fed the mixture to an air-breathing engine. If they had put a combustion chamber in there, between the wheels and heated the fuel–air mixture, they would have had the jet engine.

But if anybody did grasp this simple next step, there is no record of it; the final crucial connection was not made. 'Just dumb, just dumb', was Moss's reply to those bold enough to ask him why he just missed the point. It was one of the great lost opportunities of twentieth-century America, one which defines the very good from the truly great in the mysterious annals of invention.*

The armament fitted was in its day tremendous: no less than eight .50 machine guns. In his book on the Battle of Britain, Wing Commander H. R. Allen, DFC discusses at length the relative merits of the Colt .50 (as fitted to Mustangs and Thunderbolts) and the Browning .303 as fitted to Spitfires and Hurricanes in the Battle of Britain.**

To summarise his conclusions: the .50 Colts in batteries of four (the Thunderbolt had eight guns) were *fifteen* times more effective than eight Browning .303s. Range was doubled and in addition explosive and armour-piercing ammunition was available. He concludes that it was the .50 colts – in batteries of four – that swept the Luftwaffe from the skies of Europe. Thus the eight guns of the Thunderbolt were if anything an overkill weapon – more than capable of shooting down any aircraft of that era with a short burst. To all this could be added 2,500lb of bombs or ten 5in rockets! Thus, a pair of P-47s had at least the same bombing power as a B-17, as well as their own devastating firepower.

Ultimately, much of the appeal of this aircraft must be because of its size and power. A machine like this looks and sounds impressive. The human imagination can grasp its power and respond to the almost lifelike quality of its engine under different loads: starting, tickover, taxiing, take-off and flight. Designed by engineers of genius – in this case primarily Alexander Kartveli – using judgement, experience, imagination and slide rules, this was no aerospace winged rocket born of a number-crunching computer. The hand of craftsmanship and the eye of the artist bestowed a vital spirit, a spark of life, thereby striking a resonant chord deep within us.

Many Thunderbolts have colourful markings and camouflage which also adds to the attractiveness of the type. Not only are they attractive in themselves but they are also evocative. Any American aircraft of World War II surrounded by jeeps and men in uniforms, leather jackets and helmets conjures up a whole 'frontier' atmosphere and ethos; and for the aviation enthusiast, aircraft like the Thunderbolt typify this feeling. The attraction remains, and, hopefully, they will fly on into the twenty-first century lovingly preserved by enthusiasts.

SILVER WARRIORS *Robert Watts*
24 × 36in (61 × 91.5cm), oil on linen.

In this fine study Robert Watts has chosen to portray the Thunderbolt in unpainted finish – save for national markings. At the angle the artist has posed the aircraft, the shape of the wings and tail are shown to great effect. In addition, both aircraft are climbing, which adds to the feeling of motion. The two aircraft complement each other very well and create a triangular composition pointing towards the vanishing point, in turn echoed and reinforced by the river below.

The combination of cloud and land in this composition is notable in that the cloud serves as a background for the more distant aircraft and the land for the nearer one. This enhances the sense of three-dimensional space. The use of light is notable and the glinting of reflections on metal and canopies makes for an even more eye-catching study.

---

* Glyn Jones, *The Jet Pioneers* (Methuen, 1989), pp183–4.
** H. R. Allen, DFC, *Who Won the Battle of Britain!* (Panther, 1974), pp78–81.

DUXFORD PAIR *Ivan Berryman*
14 × 20in (35.5 × 51cm), acrylic on canvas.

This is a very attractive and flattering study of two
P-47 D-25s of the 82nd Fighter Squadron, 78th Fighter
Wing, based at Duxford in 1944. Drab-green P-47Ds were
quite rare, but these were among the first 25 delivered
with the bubble-hood, as evidenced by the -25 suffix.
(Power plant was the Pratt and Whitney R-2800-59.)

The painting poses both aircraft at their best. By
composing the picture as he has, Berryman enhances the
appearance of both machines, not only by their pose but
also by the shape created by the space between them. This
space, less on canvas than the depth of the nearest aircraft's
fuselage, together with the perspective effect imparts an
added feeling of depth to the picture.

Both aircraft are beginning a gentle turn. This avoids
any static feel and gives a feeling of space, light and speed.
The cloud serves as a horizon line while high above in the
stratosphere wisps of cirrus cloud create a reference point
for the eye, suggesting immense height.

Although in olive drab and invasion (of Europe) stripes,
the aircraft glint and sparkle in the very bright light. Their
chequered engine cowlings almost give them racing-car
like appearance and convey to us instantly the élan of the
United States Army Air Force.

'There are two ways of painting warplanes: you can
make them seem menacing and purposeful, or you
can portray them as things of great beauty. I prefer
the latter, affording them dignity and grace while at
the same time carefully observing authenticity.

I am not sure that many would refer to Republic's
P-47 as a 'pretty' aeroplane (if you are not careful as
an artist, you can make it look like a cement mixer
from any angle!), but I think that the 'D' variants
were all a huge improvement aesthetically over the
earlier 'razor-backs', being a pared-down, slender
version of their precursors.'

IVAN BERRYMAN

CALM BEFORE THE STORM *Jim Laurier*
20 × 32in (51 × 81.5cm), oil on masonite.

Although a tubby aeroplane, certain views give the P-47 a most graceful aspect and here Jim Laurier has certainly caught it to the best effect. We can see the lovely curves of the wings and tailplane and, at this angle, the elliptical shape of the cowling is clearly visible.

This is a picture which because it tells a story – the ground-crew's story – draws us into the scene. The many boxes of .50 calibre ammunition to feed the eight guns, drop tanks, numerous items to be checked and serviced:

the ground-crew are fighting every bit as much as the pilot in the cockpit, without them not one aircraft would fly.

The Crew Chiefs were usually sergeants; these men knew that even the simplest task, such as wiping the windscreen, could make just the difference between success and failure, living and dying.

The colour in this painting is very atmospheric and attractive. The aircraft camouflage and markings are arresting to the eye. The 'Star and Bar', a powerful symbol, is set off by the otherwise dull camouflage. The early-morning light glints in the cockpit canopy and we sense the rising tension before the day's mission begins.

'These are 62nd Squadron P-47s of the 56th Fighter Group. I chose to depict the early-morning activities of the ground-crews – arming, fuelling, cleaning and making last-minute checks of everything on their ship before turning her over to the pilot. It will not be long before the whole airfield roars to life as many machines of war claw their way into the sky to do battle. While the pilots received all the publicity, it is important to know that for each aircraft and pilot there were several ground-crew members. Little has been said or done to thank them for their considerable efforts to keep their aircraft in top condition. It was not a small responsibility because many lives depended on their work – not just the pilots'. Without them, probably not one aeroplane would ever have lifted off the ground to fight in the skies.'

JIM LAURIER

STILL LIFE WITH JUG *Charles J. Thompson*
36 × 24in (91.5 × 61cm), oil.

This style of aircraft portrait – the unusual close up view – is one of the trademarks of Charles Thompson who has made it his speciality. By painting an aircraft in this way the artist challenges our thinking and forces us to see anew what might otherwise be almost too familiar: the aircraft takes on new shape and identity. For example the fuselage, which we know anyway to be wide and bulbous, from this angle looks especially so and is reminiscent of the body of a whale. Had we noticed before the way the cockpit canopy comes to a point at the rear? The curvature of the tailplane and elevators is much more pronounced when contrasted against the angularity of the fin and rudder.

But it would be a mistake to conclude that this style's only merit is to draw attention to detail otherwise missed. The artist by so doing creates a totally new and fascinating play of shape and light, thereby transforming a hitherto perhaps familiar object into something fresh and challenging. He does this not merely for effect, to create a sort of *trompe-l'oeil*, but rather to see into the aircraft with the penetrating eye of the designer and engineer. This is a view which Thompson believes gives him the greatest insight possible into the structure and aerodynamics of a design. Like the depiction of a single snowflake as a crystal, portraying an aircraft in minute detail enables us to sense its inner design and character.

The painting is notable too for the photo-realism of the technique which creates a wonderful interplay of curved shining surfaces reflecting and re-reflecting each other.

'One of my formative experiences which I recall with great clarity was when as a boy of five I was taken to the local airport to see some Vickers Valentias. I was amazed when I got close to discover that they were not solid lumps of silver metal, as they had first appeared in the air overhead, but fragile canvas-covered wooden frames. Some of this close-to tactile/smell/wonderment feeling is what I try to portray in my threequarter-rear views. Whenever I walk around an aircraft I look into the structure and design and try to see the how and why of the aircraft designer's work. I find this aspect of aircraft fascinating. Coming as I do from an automotive-styling background I have a ready appreciation and understanding of the aesthetics of design.

The P-47 is a most wonderful and fascinating aircraft, full of marvellous three-dimensional shapes which I have translated into two on canvas. This particular aircraft, being mostly polished metal, created a fascinating interplay of light and reflection which I have tried to capture.'

CHARLES THOMPSON

89

NOT MY TURN TO DIE *Jim Laurier*
26 × 30in (66 × 76cm), oil on canvas.

In aviation art exciting and heroic incidents are a favourite theme and this picture portrays one such during World War II. Unable to bail out because of a jammed canopy the wounded pilot, Robert Johnson, was forced to remain in his crippled aircraft. Because the P-47 was so strongly built the Focke-Wulf 190 pilot failed to shoot him down. Eventually, possibly out of ammunition, the German pilot flew alongside his adversary and saluted before flying off.

This rare moment of chivalry permits the sort of composition normally seen only at a latter-day air display. It did, however, actually occur. The picture gives us an opportunity to compare the lines of the P-47 Thunderbolt with those of the early-model Focke-Wulf 190 with its BMW radial engine. The former is a heavyweight, the latter by comparison an equally formidable middleweight: two different design approaches to similar problems.

Apart from the highly unusual nature of the incident, the picture is an interesting one because it shows off well the solid lines of the razor-back P-47.

Robert S. Johnson returned from this mission safely, became a top-scoring ace and went on to survive the war.

'On 26 June 1943 Robert S. Johnson was still a 'green' combat pilot. He eventually became one of the highest-scoring aces in US Air Force history and certainly one of the finest fighter pilots America has produced. Bob Johnson scored an impressive 28 aerial victories, all but two of his victims being single-seat fighter aircraft, while flying with the notorious 56th Fighter Group known as "Zemke's Wolfpack". The Wolfpack was to the Luftwaffe what Richtofen's Flying Circus was to the Allied pilots of World War I. Their white-nosed Thunderbolts became known and respected by German pilots and soon achieved one of the highest tallies of enemy aircraft destroyed by an 8th Airforce fighter group.

On this day, while escorting bombers into Germany, Johnson was hit by German fighters from above. He was unable to open the canopy and bail out due to the nature of the damage, so, wounded and with a crippled aeroplane, he set course for England. A Focke-Wulf 190 caught up with him and tried repeatedly to finish him off without success. Finally the German pulled up close and saluted him before heading home.

After reading this passage in Bob Johnson's book *Thunderbolt* I thought it presented a good opportunity to portray two famous aircraft from opposing forces flying side by side – an extremely rare occurence.'

JIM LAURIER

THUNDERBOLT MK II *Michael Turner*
12 × 16in (30.5 × 40.5cm), gouache.

This painting of a Thunderbolt in RAF service depicts a Mk II (P-47D) of 134 Squadron in Burma late in 1945.

The artist has caught the monsoon weather with its brooding skies portending a storm in both a meteorological and a military sense. The P-47 is a bird of the storm, sweeping from the skies to rain down the 'thunderbolts' from which its name derives. As we can see this machine is indeed loaded with two high explosive 'bolts' – one under each wing.

The spray being thrown up from the taxi-way by the slipstream from the propeller gives a tangible sense of power akin to a steam-producing locomotive. The discarded oil-drum and the pierced metal sheeting serving to provide a stable runway suggest a makeshift forward airfield. Here is the very edge of the aerial front-line and these aircraft are clearly supporting advancing troops.

Overhead two aircraft in formation climb away from the aerodrome showing off the lovely wing planform of the Thunderbolt.

This atmospheric picture lets us see a somewhat unusual but fascinating setting for the Thunderbolt – RAF service in the Far East; an aspect of this outstanding aircraft's service often overlooked.

RETURN TO HALESWORTH *Gil Cohen*
22 × 44in (56 × 112cm), oil.

This is a most atmospheric picture where the aircraft has become part of the group. It is both the setting for the interaction we are seeing between pilot (Captain Walker M. Mahurin of the 56th Fighter Group) and ground-crew and also a part of it.

The artist has positioned the aircraft such that the cockpit beckons us invitingly, and the crew chief standing on the wing seems ready to help strap us in. Any enthusiast who has walked past line-ups at air shows will identify with that secret longing.

This P-47 is a razor-back; one of the earlier models with the framed sliding hood and a rear fuselage with a razor-like edge that, together with the rounded shape of the tailplane and elevators, gives it a rather late-1930s pre-war feel (compare this with the more angular Mustang which

set a style still with us today in trainers and light aircraft).

The composition is enhanced by the use of light and shade – silhouetting aircraft, pilot and crew against a sunset sky. Equally, the group of figures to the left is counterbalanced by the aircraft's fin and rudder to the right, and in the distance, other P-47s also help to frame them.

This is a most evocative study of flying in what many believe was its heyday, when leather helmets and goggles, together with aircraft designed and flown by people rather than computers, were the very stuff of romantic dreams.

P-47D THUNDERBOLT, 82nd FIGHTER SQUADRON *Ernest Nisbet*
14 × 17in (35.5 × 43cm), gouache.

This striking painting is very interesting for a number of different reasons. The use of colour is very bold; the deep blue of a clear high-altitude sky serves as a perfect backdrop for the natural aluminium finish of the B-17Gs, and equally the olive drab P-47D, which is the main subject in this picture. This dramatic contrast is further enhanced by the chequered pattern on the engine cowling of the P-47D. The artist has carefully picked out the very bright highlights on the upper fuselages of the B-17Gs and the canopy of the P-47D.

Any feeling of static illustration is dispelled by the way all three aircraft are inclined one toward the other in slight climbing/descending attitudes. The condensation trails from the B-17s add to the feeling of speed.

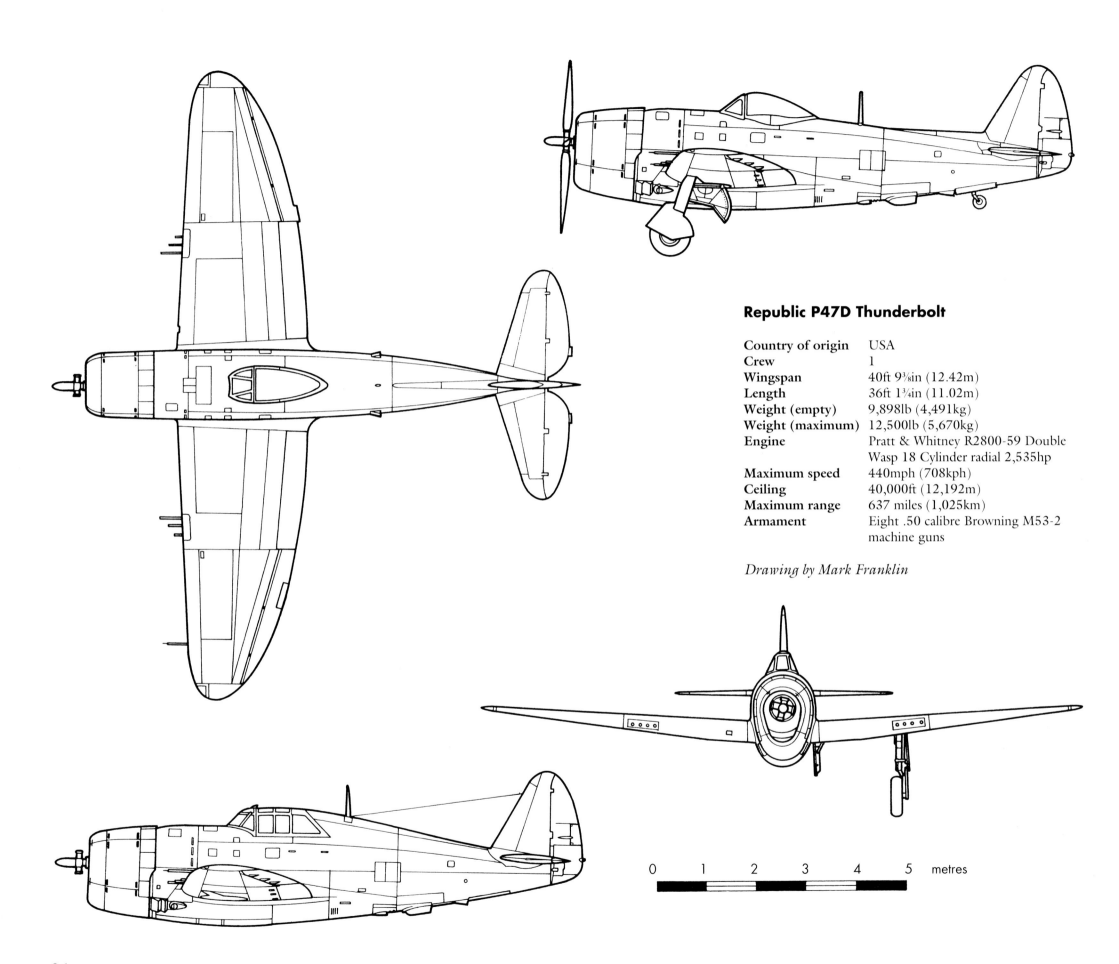

Republic **P47D Thunderbolt**

Country of origin	USA
Crew	1
Wingspan	40ft 9⅜in (12.42m)
Length	36ft 1¾in (11.02m)
Weight (empty)	9,898lb (4,491kg)
Weight (maximum)	12,500lb (5,670kg)
Engine	Pratt & Whitney R2800-59 Double Wasp 18 Cylinder radial 2,535hp
Maximum speed	440mph (708kph)
Ceiling	40,000ft (12,192m)
Maximum range	637 miles (1,025km)
Armament	Eight .50 calibre Browning M53-2 machine guns

Drawing by Mark Franklin

0 1 2 3 4 5 metres

BIBLIOGRAPHY

AVIATION ART

Batchelor, John & Christy (1985) *Illustration in Action: How to Draw and Paint Aircraft, Ships and Vehicles*, Blandford.

Blake, J. (1991) *Gerald Coulson: The Masterworks*, David & Charles.

Donne, Michael, OBE (1986) *A Lifetime of Aviation 1916–1986*, Society of Aerospace Manufacturers and Ducimus Books.

Handleman, Philip (1992) *Aviation: A History Through Art*, Howell Press, USA.

Larkin, David (1976) *Aviation Art of Frank Wootton*, Peacock Bantam.

Thompson, Charles (1990) *Wings*, Pan.

Turner, Michael (1986) *Luftwaffe Aircraft*, Temple Press.

Valdivia, Mary Henderson (1984) *At Home in the Sky, Aviation Art of Frank Wootton*, Smithsonian Press.

Walker, C. & Taylor, R. (1991) *Robert Taylor: Air Combat Paintings Volume II*, David & Charles.

Weston, R. & Taylor, R. (1987) *The Air Combat Paintings of Robert Taylor*, David & Charles.

Wootton, Frank (1992) *Frank Wootton: 50 Years of Aviation Art*, David & Charles.

Young, J. (1990) *The Aviation Paintings of John Young*, David & Charles.

SPITFIRE

Air Ministry Pilot's Notes (1972) *Supermarine Spitfire VI*, Air Data Publications.

Ashman, R. V. (1989) *Spitfire Against the Odds: Memoirs of a Fighter Pilot*, Patrick Stephens.

Bader, Douglas (1989) *Fight for the Sky: Story of the Spitfire and Hurricane*, Sidgwick & Jackson.

Bowyer, Michael J. F. (1986) *Spitfire: Fifty Years On*, Patrick Stephens.

Burns, Michael (1986) *Spitfire! Spitfire!*, Blandford Press.

Dicks, Terrance (1991) *Spitfire Summer*, Red Fox.

Flack, Jeremy (1992) *Spitfire: The Legend Lives On*, Osprey.

Green, David (1991) *Spitfires Reborn*, Brooks Books.

Griffiths, Harry (1992) *Testing Times: Memoirs of a Spitfire Boffin*, United Writers Publications.

Haining, Peter (1989) *Spitfire Log*, Futura.

Hamilton, James Douglas (1990) *Air Battle for Malta: Diaries of a Spitfire Pilot*, Airlife Publications.

Henshaw, Alex (1990) *Sigh for a Merlin*, Arrow Books.

Hooton, E. R. (1969) *Supermarine Spitfire Mk. I-XVI in RAF, SAAF, RAAF, RNZAF, RCAF and Foreign Service*, Aircam Aviation.

Johnstone, Sandy (1988) *Spitfire into War*, Grafton Books.

Kelly, Terence (1988) *Hurricane and Spitfire Pilots at War*, Arrow Books.

Morgan, Eric B. & Shacklady, Edward (1987) *Spitfire: The History*, Key Publications.

Neil, T. F. (1990) *From the Cockpit: Spitfire*, Ian Allan.

Olmsted, Bill (1989) *Blue Skies: The Autobiography of a Canadian Spitfire Pilot in World War II*, Stoddart, Canada.

Price, Alfred (1991) *Spitfire: A Complete Fighting History*, Paperboards Promotional Reprint Co.

Price, Alfred (1992) *Spitfire Story*, Arms & Armour Press.

Quill, Jeffrey (1983) *Spitfire: A Test Pilot's Story*, J. Murray.

Quill, Jeffrey (1986) *Spitfire: A Test Pilot's Story*, Arrow Books.

Quill, Jeffrey & Cox, Sebastian (1986) *Birth of a Legend: Spitfire*,
Quiller Publications.

Quill, Jeffrey & Cox, Sebastian (1987) *Birth of a Legend: Spitfire*, Quiller Publications.

Rimmell, Raymond (1985) *Spitfire: Supermarine Spitfire Mk. V, Aeroguide*, Linewrights.

Rouse, Waly (1989) *Born Again: Spitfire PS 915*, Midland Counties Publications.

Russell, C. R. (1985) *Spitfire Odyssey: My Life at Supermarines, 1936–57*, Kingfisher.

Sarkar, Dilip (1992) *Invisible Thread: Spitfire's Tale*, Ramrod Publications.

Shores, Christopher *et al* (1991) *Malta: The Spitfire Year, 1942*, Grub Street.

Slack, Tom (1987) *Happy is the Day: Spitfire Pilot's Story*, United Writers Publications.

Smith, Duncan (1990) *Spitfire into Battle*, Arrow Books.

Spick, Mike (1990) *Spitfire: Classic War Planes*, Salamander Books.

Steinhilper, Ulrich, Osborne, Peter & Osborne, Carol (1990) *Spitfire on My Tail: A View from the Other Side*, Independent Books.

Ward, John (1986) *Spitfire and Hurricane Tribute: Royal Airforce Battle of Britain Memorial Flight*, Ian Allan.

LANCASTER

Air Ministry Pilot's Notes (1972) *Avro Lancaster*, Air Data Publications.

Brickhill, Paul (1984) *The Dambusters*, Bell and Hyman.

Garbett & Goulding (1992) *Lancaster at War Vols I–IV*, Ian Allan.

Mason, Francis K. (1989) *Avro Lancaster*, Aston Publications.

Rimmell, Raymond L. (1986) *Lancaster: Avro Lancaster B Mk. 1*, Aeroguide Classics, Linewrights.

Sweetman, John (1992) *Dambuster Raid*, Arms and Armour Press.

Wood, D. C. (Ed.) (1991) *Design and Development of the Avro Lancaster*, Royal Aeronautical Society.

FORTRESS B-17

Air Ministry Pilot's Notes (1972) *Boeing Fortress (B-17)*, Air Data Publications.

Bowman, Martin W. (1992) *Flying to Glory: B-17 Flying Fortress in War and Peace*, Patrick Stephens.

Freeman, Roger (1990) *B-17 Flying Fortress: Combat Profiles*, Ian Allan.

Kinzey, B. (1982) *B-17 Flying Fortress: Pt. 1, Detail & Scale*, Aero.

Kinzey, B. (1986) *B-17 Flying Fortress: Pt. 3*, Aero.

Lloyd, A. T. (1983) *B-17 Flying Fortress: Pt. 2, Derivatives, Detail & Scale*, Aero.

McDowell, Ernest R. (1987) *Flying Fortress: Boeing B-17*, Squadron/Signal Publications, USA.

O'Leary, Michael (1992) *B-17 Flying Fortress*, Osprey.

Richardson, Doug (1991) *Boeing B-17 Flying Fortress, Classic War Planes*, Salamander Books.

MESSERSCHMITT 109

Aero Series (1965) *Messerschmitt Me 109*, Aero.

Beaman, J. B. (1983) *Messerschmitt Bf109 In Action, Pt. 2*, Squadron/Signal Publications, USA.

Green, William (1987) *Augsburg Eagle, Messerschmitt Bf109*, Aston Publications.

Musciano, Walter A. (1990) *Messerschmitt Aces*, TAB Books, USA.

Nowarra, Heinz J. (1989) *Messerschmitt Me109: Aircraft and Legend*, Paperboards GT Foulis.

Nowarra, Heinz J. (1991) *Messerschmitt Bf109*, Schiffer, USA.

Payne, Michael (1987) *Messerschmitt Bf109 into the Battle*, Kristall Productions.

Price, Alfred (1992) *Messerschmitt Bf109: Classic War Planes*, Paperboards Salamander Books.

Rimmel, Raymond L. (1986) *Messerschmitt Bf109E*, Aeroguide Classics, Linewrights.

P-51 MUSTANG

Davis, Larry (1982) *P-51 Mustang in Colour*, Paperboards Squadron/Signal Publications, USA.

Davis, Larry (1992) *North American P-51 Mustang: A Photo Chronicle*, Schiffer, USA.

Ethell, Jeffrey (1990) *P-51 Mustang*, Arms & Armour Press.

Famous Aircraft (1979) *P-51 Mustang*, Aero.

Freeman, Roger A. (1989) *P-51 Mustang: Combat Profiles*, Ian Allan.

Goebel, Robert J. (1991) *Mustang Ace! Memoirs of a P-51 Fighter Pilot*, Pacifica, USA.

Gunston, Bill (1990) *P-51 Mustang, Classic War Planes*, Salamander Books.

Wagner, Ray (1991) *Mustang Designer: Edgar Schmued and the Development of the P-51*, Crown Publishers.

P-47 THUNDERBOLT

Freeman, Roger A. (1978) *Thunderbolt: A Documentary History of the Republic P-47*, Macdonald & J.

Freeman, Roger A. (1992) *Thunderbolt: A Documentary History of the Republic P-47*, Arms & Armour Press.

Hagedorn, D. (1992) *Republic P-47 Thunderbolt – The Final Chapter, Latin American Air Forces Service*, Phalanx Publishing Co, USA.

GENERAL

Allen, H. R. DFC (1976) *Who Won the Battle of Britain*, Panther.

Boyne, Walter J. (1980) *Messerschmitt Me262 Arrow to the Future*, Janes, London.

Dempster, D. and Wood, D. (1991) *Narrow Margin*, Airlife Books.

Edgerton, David (1991) *England and the Aeroplane*, McMillan.

Jones, Glyn (1989) *The Jet Pioneers*, Methuen.

Mason, Derek (1969) *Battle over Britain*, McWhirter.

GUILDS AND SOCIETIES

All listed are open to non-artist members and have newsletters, exhibitions and regular meetings and shows.

U.K.

Guild of Aviation Artists
Secretary: Hugo Trotter, Unit 516 Bondway Business Centre, 71 Bondway, Vauxhall Cross, London SW8 1SQ
The Manchester Aviation Art Society meets 1st Tuesday every month at The Air & Space Museum, Castlefield, Deansgate, Manchester.

U.S.A.

The American Society of Aviation Artists
Secretary: Luther Gore, 1805 Meadowbrook Heights Road, Charlottesville, Virginia 22901, U.S.A.

INDEX

Page references in *italics* indicate illustrations